A Fresh
Vision *of* Jesus

# A Fresh
# Vision *of* Jesus

*Timeless Ways to Experience Christ*

## CHERI FULLER

Revell

Grand Rapids, Michigan

© 2005 by Cheri Fuller

Published by Fleming H. Revell
a division of Baker Publishing Group
P.O. Box 6287, Grand Rapids, MI 49516-6287

Printed in the United States of America

Library of Congress Cataloging-in-Publication Data
Fuller, Cheri.
    A fresh vision of Jesus : timeless ways to experience Christ / Cheri Fuller.
        p.    cm.
    Includes bibliographical references.
    ISBN 0-8007-5853-6  (pbk.)
        1. Christian life—Meditations. 2. Spiritual life—Christianity—Meditations.
    I. Title.
    BV4501.3.F848 2005
    232—dc22                                                      2004015135

For reasons of privacy, some names used in this book have been changed.

To
Peggy and Earl Stewart,
our dear friends and prayer partners,
through whom we see the joy and love of Jesus
again and again

# Contents

Acknowledgments    9

1. Seeing Jesus    11

**Part 1  A Fresh Vision of Jesus through the Word**
2. The Living Word    23
3. The Psalms Prescription    33
4. Words That Changed a Life    44
5. A Vision That Endures    53

**Part 2  A Fresh Vision of Jesus through Service**
6. The Bread of Life    65
7. The Face of Jesus    74
8. An Expectant Heart    82
9. Jehovah Is Still God    90

**Part 3  A Fresh Vision of Jesus through Trials**
10. Climbing into God's Lap    101
11. The Lord Who Sees Me    109
12. I've Just Seen Jesus!    117
13. The Joy of Obedience    124

**Part 4  A Fresh Vision of Jesus through Mountaintop Experiences**

14. The Great Physician  135
15. A Light in the Darkness  145
16. The Road to Emmaus  155
17. The Trysting Place  163

**Part 5  A Fresh Vision of Jesus through His Whispers**

18. The Lord Our Reconciler  175
19. Can You Hear My Voice?  185
20. The Power of His Word  194
21. The Miracle of His Presence  204

Notes  215

# Acknowledgments

I am deeply grateful to those who have prayed for me during the writing of this book, especially Peggy and Earl Stewart, Janet Page, Jo Hayes, Betsy West, Elaine Shaw, Melina Shellenberger, Anne Denmark, and Jocelyn Obermeyer. And I'm always grateful for Flo Perkins's prayers, which are still being answered although she's already in heaven. Each of you has laid the tracks for God's power to come through this book as you have prayed, and I thank you from my heart.

Thanks to those people who have allowed me to share stories about God working in their lives, including Pam Alley, Terri Geary, Richard Drake, and Earl Stewart. I especially thank my son, Justin, for his graciousness and am grateful to my sister Martha for allowing me to share her story of reconciliation and hope. And I'm ever grateful for those Christians from the past who have mentored and inspired me through their books and memoirs: Hannah Hurnard, Hannah Whitall Smith, Corrie ten Boom, Amy Carmichael, and Gladys Aylward.

Much appreciation to Suzie Eller for her insight and writing assistance, which helped the biblical narratives of this book come to life, to Melanie Hemry and Victorya Rogers for being iron sharpening iron, and to my daughter-in-law Maggie for her editorial help in revisions.

Thank you, Vicki Crumpton, for being a terrific editor, and thanks to the Revell team for all that you have done to get this book into readers' hands. Working with all of you is a joy.

I am so grateful for our five grandchildren—Luke, Josephine, Noah, Caleb, and Caitlin—who light up my life and keep me inspired. To your parents Justin and Tiff, Chris and Maggie, and Ali and Hans, and most of all to Holmes, who is my constant supporter, prayer partner, traveling companion, and husband—I love you.

# ONE

# Seeing Jesus

*Seeing Jesus is what Christianity is all about. Mark it
down. We are what we see. . . . Acquiring a vision of
your Maker can be like starting a whole new life.*
                                        MAX LUCADO

I lifted my face to the dazzling September sun. My husband, Holmes, and I were as excited as a couple of kids
before a birthday party. We had tickets for a "Balmy
Day" ride. The brochure bragged, "Maine's favorite ocean
day trip—enjoy a quiet boat ride to Monhegan Island—the
experience will be your vacation highlight!"

As inlanders we didn't even think to check the marine fore-cast. The sun was shining. It was windy, but it's windy lots of days where we live, so we didn't worry.

"Are you *sure* you want to go?" the ticket agent at the dock asked me. "Tomorrow's going to be a better day."

That should have given me a clue—but I forged ahead. "Today's our only chance. We have to fly back to Oklahoma tomorrow," I told her.

"It's going to be bumpy out there. I could refund your money," she added. I picked up our tickets anyway and got us egg sandwiches and coffee across the street, and Holmes and I boarded the *Balmy Days II* at pier number eight with a group of other brave but naïve folks.

Before we were out of the harbor, the young woman behind me was popping Dramamine. She offered me some. "I don't get motion sickness, but thanks!" I told her with a smile.

About halfway to the island, I began to taste that egg sand-wich and wish I'd taken her up on the offer of Dramamine. "Don't worry," the first mate said over the intercom, "it'll be smoother on the way back."

After an hour we arrived at Monhegan. For a few hours we walked around the island, strolling through art galleries and eating a picnic lunch on the big hill with a spectacular view of the ocean. Then we boarded the boat again, hoping for a smooth ride back to Boothbay.

We were only a few minutes out of the harbor when the gentle rocking intensified. Soon I felt myself slam from side to side as I gripped the rail with white knuckles. Just as I readied myself for the next wave, the boat lurched forward, and I almost lost my seat. The boat pitched down and rolled from side to side as it moved into the wind and waves.

Every muscle in my body tensed as the cold water blowing in the cabin door splattered my sunglasses and left my hair plastered to my head. I thought each looming wave might wash us into the frigid depths.

Suddenly I heard a woman on the top deck screaming in terror. The big man groaning behind me got sick all over the deck. The woman in front of me turned a grayish green as she lay down and held on for dear life—and she was a seasoned island resident.

The captain had to steer farther out to sea in a fruitless endeavor to find calmer waters. As waves continued to crash into the boat and splash over the bow, I looked up at the life jackets, wondering if we'd have to use them. A man near me saw my glance and said, "They wouldn't help us much. The water's only forty degrees."

I realized I was gripping the bench as if *I* were the one steering the boat. Anxiety rising, I had what I could only describe as a deep connection with God. Fear, I've found, can be a great motivator to draw near to God and a powerful way to experience some intimate moments with him.

*You made this wind and the waves and you could quiet them down just like you did for the disciples!* I prayed silently.

I've experienced dozens of moments in my life when I wished things would calm down and problems would disappear. I kept on with this line of conversation with the Lord for a while, until it was clear the waves were *not* getting smaller. In fact, the boat was heaving even more.

*Then since you're not quieting the waves, would you speak to me? Quiet my heart and show me what you want me to learn.* I waited and listened.

*"Enjoy the ride,"* God seemed to say.

*Enjoy the ride?* I asked. Surely I heard wrong.

But again the words came: *"Enjoy the ride!"*

My husband, I noticed, *was* enjoying the ride—even soaking wet and cold from the waves that splashed over the top deck (of course, he also loves jumping out of airplanes).

As I pondered God's words, I looked around the lower cabin to see who else seemed to be enjoying the ride. I finally spotted an old couple, tall and ruddy-faced, who looked perfectly peaceful, as if they were on a happy Sunday excursion.

I inched my way to the back of the cabin, holding on as the boat rolled through its audition for *The Perfect Storm.*

"You look like you're really enjoying this. You don't seem scared or sick. What's your secret?" I asked the elderly pair.

"Just keep your eyes on the horizon. Don't look at the waves. Look out as far as you can. Keep your eyes peeled on the horizon way out there," they said, pointing into the distance.

Returning to my seat, I took their advice. I discovered something amazing. A sense of peace replaced my anxiety, and I began to experience Jesus as my Prince of Peace in a real way. It was almost as if I could see him on the deck smiling, reveling in his creation, and reigning over the whole excursion.

And as I got a fresh vision of Jesus and kept my eyes on the horizon, I felt his peace that afternoon. The waves didn't change. They were just as choppy, and the boat still pitched and rolled wildly.

But something in *me* changed. I experienced such a strange and wonderful calm that I went out on the deck and enjoyed the splash of the ocean water on my face. I noticed how the sun was sparkling like diamonds on the water and how gorgeous the day was. I chatted with fellow travelers. A former

Navy officer told me about the forty-five-foot waves that had rushed over the deck of the navy ship he was on in the Atlantic during World War II. To him, these ten-foot waves were child's play. "It's all about perspective," he told me.

I reveled in the gulls flying over us in the bright blue Maine sky and the school of dolphins jumping in the choppy waters near the boat. We eventually made it back to the pier, and as I look back now, the ride really *was* the highlight of our trip.

The Christian life is rarely a calm harbor ride. It's more like an adventurous ocean excursion where the waves can be huge and the ride can be bumpy and uncertain or wild and difficult. Things can seem overwhelming. Sometimes we long for calmer waters or just want to get off the boat.

Still God says, "*Look at me,* not the waves. Fix your eyes on Jesus—and don't forget to *enjoy the ride!*" (see Heb. 12:2). Our tumultuous boat ride reminds me of a card I once saw. It pictured a hippopotamus in a boat surrounded by huge waves, and inside it said:

> Lord, thank you for upheaval,
> For rocking my little boat.
> For sending winds that seem too strong
> And waves that threaten to capsize me.
> Because all of this drives me into your arms.
> And anything which results in that end, Lord,
> Is worth getting wet over.

Being driven into the arms of Jesus, I've found, is truly worth getting wet over and even worth going through a tumultuous storm now and then.

## Catching a Fresh Vision of Jesus

Staying focused on God in stressful times is a vital part of our spiritual journey. World-class sports stars such as cyclist Lance Armstrong, tennis champion Venus Williams, gymnast Shannon Miller, and golfer Tiger Woods have been the subject of research by scientists trying to determine why these stars win championships against athletes who have just as much talent and skill. What is their secret? It's not just that they practiced a lot or set aside distractions to hone their skills. So did the other athletes. *It is their ability to stay focused under stress.* They focus on a yellow jersey, a tennis championship, an Olympic gold medal, or a golf grand slam.

The Bible tells us the supreme prize is "the prize for which God, through Christ Jesus, is calling us up to heaven" (Phil. 3:14). This verse tells us what our focus is to be—something more important than winning the Tour de France or gaining the title of world champion: knowing Jesus and following him as he calls us from glory to glory.

Looking for God at every turn—and getting a fresh vision of who he is—keeps us focused on our purpose in life regardless of how rocky the journey is. Seeing and encountering Jesus isn't just something we "want"—like sprinkles on a cake's icing—it's something we *need,* something vital to a life of faith.

Our spiritual eyesight so easily becomes foggy, clouded by disappointments or marred by difficult circumstances. Sometimes we're so focused on ourselves we can't see anyone or anything else. We begin to think the Christian life is all about us instead of all about God. Often we're like the disciples on the stormy sea, with our eyes fixed on the trials and tumultuous waves that threaten to sink our ship. I love what Anne Graham Lotz said about this: "When we are faced with great problems, our tendency is to focus on the hands of God—what He has not done for us and what we want Him to do for us—instead of focusing on the face of God—simply who He is. Our depression can deepen through this kind of self-preoccupation. Often, in the midst of great problems, we stop short of the real blessing God has for us, which is a fresh vision of who He is."[1]

Sometimes our view of God is colored by old attitudes and impressions of him or perceived through the filter of our childhood experiences or the intensity of our present pain, as we'll see in the chapters ahead. And just as a marriage can get stale to the point that we walk past our mate day after day and hardly notice him, we often live without noticing the Lord, even if we've been Christians a long time. We lose the vision of his majesty, of his incredible loving-kindness, and of the richness of his mercy, and we have a hard time staying connected. We can attend church services regularly and miss seeing Jesus.

Oswald Chambers said, "Being saved and seeing Jesus are not the same thing. Many are partakers of God's grace who have never seen Jesus. When once you have seen Jesus, you can never be the same, other things do not appeal as they used to do. . . . If you have a vision of Jesus as He is, experiences can come and go, you will endure 'as seeing Him Who is invisible.'"[2]

This book is all about catching a fresh vision of Jesus and letting that vision transform your life. Most of us don't need another program to attend at church or more committee meetings, conferences, or Bible software as much as we need a fresh revelation of Christ. Because when we see Jesus, *we are changed!* Our hearts are renewed, and we are energized to continue on God's path. Second Corinthians 3:18 says, "We all, with unveiled face, beholding as in a mirror the glory of the Lord, are being transformed into the same image from glory to glory, just as from the Lord, the Spirit" (NASB).

When we see him, even a glimpse, "we are transfigured much like the Messiah, our lives gradually becoming brighter and more beautiful as God enters our lives and we become like Him" (2 Cor. 3:18 MESSAGE). Seeing Jesus clearly changes us—it changes our behavior, our relationships, and our goals.

I invite you to join me as we look at five pathways through which we can get a fresh vision of Jesus: through moments in the Word, through service, through our trials, through mountaintop experiences and events that light a fire in us, and through whispers from God's Spirit. These lead to times of repentance, hearing him more clearly, and most of all—seeing our Savior.

These pathways make up the five sections of this book. In each section you will read a story from my life, a contemporary story, and a biblical person's story. Throughout history, many believers have been transformed by a vision of Christ. Therefore, each section will include a classic or historical story. Each chapter will also include personal application points to encourage you in gaining a fresh vision of Jesus in your own life.

In the pages ahead we're going to look at ways not only to see Jesus in our everyday lives but also to fix our eyes upon him. Before you begin, here are some ways to get focused for the journey:

*Reflect.* Respond to these questions by journaling or discussing them with someone:

- When was the last time you had a real encounter with Jesus? How did this affect you or impact your life?
- What's the biggest hindrance to your spiritual journey?
- What comes into your mind when you think about God?
- When difficulties or storms hit your life, what do you tend to focus on?

*Ask.* The Bible encourages us to ask, seek, and knock (see Matt. 7:7). Tell God you want to see him as he really is right in the midst of your mundane circumstances or the chaos of your life. This kind of seeking—looking for the face of God, not just facts about God, and for God himself, not just for what he can do for us—is no small thing. God loves a relentless seeker! He promises that those who seek him will find him: "If you look for me in earnest, you will find me when you seek me. I will be found by you" (Jer. 29:13–14).

PART 1

# A Fresh Vision
# *of* Jesus through
# the Word

TWO

# The Living Word

*For the word of God is full of living power.*

HEBREWS 4:12

I sat midway down the third row in a classroom full of college freshmen shuffling papers and chattering nervously as the professor strolled into Religion 101. Dr. Anderson was heralded as one of the finest, most intellectual professors in the department, and I couldn't wait to hear him teach.

Although I'd grown up in a mainline church and answered an altar call at age twelve, I had wrestled with questions about faith and Christianity for years. Even the countless sermons I'd sat through hadn't addressed the many issues I wondered about, like: *Are heaven and hell really real? Is God a good God? If he is real and he's good, how can I really know him? Does he hear our prayers and answer them, or is it just a religious exercise we're supposed to do? Is the Bible true or just a great book of stories? Is Jesus God or just a great man that we are to emulate?*

I'd started the "Daily Bible Readings" recommended by our youth pastor so many times with great intentions, especially after mountaintop experiences at summer youth camp, only to have them become dry and lifeless after a few weeks. The pursuits of high school like drill team, boyfriends, AP courses, and applying to college reclaimed my focus.

*Now I can really get into the Bible. Now I can get answers to my questions,* I thought as I leaned forward in my chair. Dr. Anderson greeted us, opened his lecture notes, and outlined the semester. Then, with thrilling description and characterization, he told the stories of Adam and Eve and Noah and the flood from Genesis. We listened with rapt attention to his colorful rendition of the familiar narratives. At the end of the hour-and-a-half-long class, he closed his notebook and looked out at me and the other impressionable college students with his piercing blue eyes.

"What's most important to remember is that these and all the other stories in the Bible are merely myths which reveal to us the meaning of our lives. Although they represent truth, these symbolic stories existed in ancient religions that predate the religion of the Israelites by thousands of years. Through metaphorical language, these myths make intelligible what is beyond words. They represent spiritual experience but cannot be taken literally. Forget your preconceived ideas from what you've been told about these stories in childish Sunday school applications of the Bible. I want to shake you out of your complacency."

I don't know about the other students, but I was definitely shaken out of my complacency. I had already been disappointed in God's handling of things when my father dropped dead of a heart attack, my aunt drowned, and a close friend died in an accident. Now with every word the professor spoke that semester another brick in my already-faltering faith came toppling down. As the weeks wore on, the more he analyzed and lectured, the more I questioned the reality and truth of the Bible and who God is. Oh, I still attended church now and then when a friend wanted to go, but I silently disdained the "Bible thumpers" who attended Bible studies and participated in inner-city missions on the weekends while we were going to fraternity parties.

Yet God, who meets us right where we are and pursues us because he loves us even when we are still sinners, saw the yearning in my heart. He saw the pain, the confusion, and the longing to know him and began drawing me back to him in large part through the thing I spent the most time in—the study of literature.

As an English major, I loved all the courses required for the degree: American literature, British poetry, continental drama, Chaucer, Shakespeare, and others. My second semester of graduate work in English literature, I signed up for a class in seventeenth-century British poetry, not knowing that the "metaphysical poets," including John Donne, George Herbert, Henry Vaughn, and others, had a passion for Christ and that their poetry reflected their vibrant relationship with him. Merely through reading and studying these writings, God drew me a little closer. I read verses such as these by Henry Vaughn:

> My soul, there is a country
> Far beyond the stars,
> Where stands a winged sentry

25

All skilful in the wars:
There, above noise and danger,
Sweet Peace sits crowned with smiles,
And One born in a manger
Commands the beauteous files.

I also began reading theologians and philosophers on my search for truth. I found my way to Paul Tournier, the Swiss psychiatrist who was a committed Christian; Dietrich Bonhoeffer, the German pastor imprisoned and later martyred for his faith by the Nazis; and Edith Schaeffer and other L'Abri writers. Quietly I read and pondered what they had written. I continued my graduate work as I had first one son and then another, and then we moved from Texas to Tulsa, Oklahoma.

## Eyes Wide Open

I sat on the brown and gold print couch in the living room of our little house on Delaware Place one afternoon, not knowing what to do with myself. I usually spent the boys' nap time studying for my oral exams, but only a few weeks before, I'd lumbered across a stage, seven months pregnant, and received my diploma. I had nothing left to study. I'd done everything that was supposed to bring happiness, or so I thought. I had gotten married after college. We had two precious little boys and one child on the way. We lived in a nice brick home with white shutters and a white picket fence on a pleasant street. I had finally even been able to buy the much-longed-for yellow country print curtains for our bedroom. I had finished my degree after working on it for five years, and Holmes was doing well in the clothing business.

26

Everything should have been fine. But at twenty-nine I found myself asking, like the old Peggy Lee song, "Is that all there is?" I had an empty place inside that none of the wonderful things and people had filled. I was worried about our son's persistent asthma attacks and beset by fears. Without a single good friend in the city we'd just moved to, I was extremely lonely. Holmes and I were so busy in our individual pursuits that we had become increasingly distant and the small, daily resentments had piled up between us like the Great Wall of China. As long as I was working toward a goal, I could keep the loneliness and fear at bay. I could stuff down the unresolved losses and pain. But a darkness seemed to be encroaching that I couldn't deny any longer.

So that afternoon as the boys slept, I combed through the bookcase looking for something worthwhile to read. Nothing looked halfway interesting.

Finally my hand hit upon a dusty Phillips translation of the New Testament my husband had used in a college class. I hadn't read the Bible in a long time, but settling myself on the couch, I began to read it in the quiet as the rain splashed on the window beside me.

I started with the book of Matthew, the first book in the New Testament, and read it page after page, chapter after chapter, day after day, just as I'd read so many books before. I finished Matthew and moved on to the book of Mark and then Luke, not missing a chapter or verse.

Several weeks later, I was ready to delve into the book of John. I read,

At the beginning God expressed himself. That personal expression, that word, was with God and was God, and he existed with God from the beginning. All creation took place through him, and none took place without him. In him appeared life and this life was the light of mankind. The light still shines in the darkness and the darkness has never put it out.

JOHN 1:1–5 PHILLIPS

As I read those words, the lights went on. I felt as if scales fell from my eyes and they were opened so I could comprehend the truth.

*That word . . . that is Jesus. He was with God from the very beginning. He created everything! Nothing was created except through him. In him, in Jesus, is LIFE, and his life is the light of all humanity.*

I was stunned as I realized that Jesus wasn't just in the past but is *now* the living Word and that he is alive in his Word, speaking to hearts today just as he did when he walked the earth. He is the light who came into the world to bring us out of darkness into his marvelous light.

*Jesus is alive!* I was so excited you'd have thought I was Mary and had just seen him appear at the tomb. Mere words can't express the explosion of truth and light that went on inside me. *He is not a myth as my professor suggested. He is not irrelevant as culture depicts him. He is not a God of the past who spun the world into existence and then left mankind to fend for ourselves, but he is Emmanuel, God with us.* An irrepressible joy filled my mind and heart, and the presence of Christ seemed all around me and within me.

At the same moment all this joy and awakening was happening, I had a sobering sense of conviction and thought, *If this is all true, if every word in the Bible is real and authentic and from God, how should I be living?* Thus began the

28

process of repentance. A new desire to read God's Word and his commandments in order to know *how* I was to live welled up in me, and from then on I read as if that little green New Testament contained all the treasures of life in its pages—which it did! The fresh vision of the Savior I was getting would transform everything in my life: my marriage, my thinking and perspective, my relationships, my career, and my mission in life.

A few days later I was driving down a Tulsa street with my children, the sense of God's presence still very real and alive. A still, small voice started addressing issues I had wondered about for a long time, like, "Heaven and hell are real and start here—which path are you choosing? Eternal life begins now, on this earth. Who will you give to your life to?" With my response of "I'm all yours, Lord—every part of me, my today, and all my tomorrows," we began a conversation that has continued to this day.

My family's problems didn't disappear just because of my spiritual renewal. In fact, our son's asthma got worse, I had active five- and three-year-olds and a newborn to care for, and three weeks after our daughter was born we moved to a new city where I didn't know anyone. But now I was aware that I did not have to handle mothering, my son's illness, the kids' earaches or chicken pox, or life itself alone anymore, and it made all the difference.

And though circumstances hadn't changed, I felt as if I had taken off dark glasses. The grass seemed an emerald green, the sky more vividly blue. I was filled with wonder and gratitude. Things I'd passed by hundreds of times—monarch butterflies, sunsets, a basket of green apples, and new days—now were amazing to me. I was awed by the marvelous gift of my children and husband and experienced a new love for them and for others around me.

I began to have an especially new love for the Bible. Struck by the relevancy in this living Word, I got up early each morning to read it, page by page, chapter by chapter, and line by line. I heard God speak to me in the verses and found it true over and over that "the Word that God speaks is alive and active; it cuts more keenly than any two-edged sword: it strikes through to the place where soul and spirit meet, to the innermost intimacies of a man's being: it examines the very thoughts and motives of a man's heart" (Heb. 4:12 PHILLIPS).

## Catching a Fresh Vision of Jesus

God reveals himself in the Bible and through Christ, the eternal Word. Jesus is the face of God, the visible image of the invisible God. Hebrews 1:3 (NIV) says, "The Son is the radiance of God's glory and the exact representation of his being, sustaining all things by his powerful word." "In the beginning (before all time) was the Word (Christ), and the Word was with God, and the Word was God himself" (John 1:1 AMP). John 1:14 says, "And the Word became flesh, and dwelt among us, and we saw His glory, glory as of the only begotten from the Father, full of grace and truth" (NASB). From Genesis to Revelation the Lord gives countless snapshots of himself. The Bible's stories are not just nice stories, not myths that are representations of truth, but "true truth,"[1] as Edith Schaeffer says, so that we can know him and come to love and worship him and surrender our lives to him. Here are some ways to know him better:

30

*Lay down false notions about God taken from culture.* I got some weird ideas about God from my religion professor. Like me, you may have acquired false notions about him from your education, the movies, or art. God has had a colorful yet flawed movie career, and sometimes the portrayals are blasphemous. Often he is portrayed more as a caricature than the Creator of the universe.

In the 1950s movie *The Ten Commandments,* God was a booming, disembodied voice. In Michelangelo's famous mural on the ceiling of the Sistine Chapel, *Creation of Adam,* God is a white-bearded strongman. In the 1980s comedy film *Oh, God!* he was a wisecracking, good-natured old man with a cigar. In the more recent movie *Dogma,* God was a raucous rock star. The hit song "From a Distance" implied that God is watching us from a long way away but doesn't have any power or involvement in our life. The latest popular incarnation of God was in the movie *Bruce Almighty,* in which God was humanized as a dignified Higher Power who sometimes posed as a janitor. "Think it's easy being the Man Upstairs?" God asks Bruce, the television reporter who's blaming God for his problems. "Then you try running the world."

Reflect on movies, books, and songs from which you've gotten ideas about God. How do these line up with stories in the Word, God's interactions with people, and how the Bible portrays him? Is his loving-kindness represented and his invitation to people to enter into a new relationship with him through Jesus Christ demonstrated?

The Bible is "a perfect picture of God. . . . One of the main reasons we have the Bible," says Josh McDowell, "is to show us what God is like. It is a revelation of God to us. And the

31

better we know him, the closer our relationship can be with him."[2]

*Read the Gospel of John for the purpose of "beholding the Lord."* Just as your body needs to be nourished with good food, your spiritual life needs fuel. Through his Word Jesus can reveal himself to you, speak to you, guide you, and encourage you.

John is a terrific book of the Bible to begin delving into because it contains some of the most basic yet profound truths about Jesus Christ. Whether you have never read the Bible, are a new believer, or have read the whole Bible before, let me encourage you to read the book of John for more than getting through a certain number of chapters in a week or verses in a sitting. Read it to "behold the Lord" as described by Madame Guyon, a Christian from sixteenth-century France. As you read, pause instead of rushing ahead to the next verse. Sit in the Lord's presence, "beholding him," and make use of the Scripture to quiet your mind. As Madame Guyon said,

The way to do this is really quite simple. First, read a passage of Scripture. Once you sense the Lord's presence, the content of what you have read is no longer important. The Scripture has served its purpose; it has quieted your mind; it has brought you to Him. . . . The Lord's chief desire is to reveal himself to you and, in order for him to do that, he gives you abundant grace. The Lord gives you the experience of enjoying his presence. He touches you, and his touch is so delightful that, more than ever, you are drawn inwardly to him.[3]

As you do this, you will not only discover wonderful truths in his Word, but you will discover anew Jesus Christ, the living Word.

# THREE

# The Psalms Prescription

*Christ is full and sufficient for all his people . . . he is a garment of righteousness to cover and adorn them; a Physician to heal them; a Counselor to advise them; a Captain to defend them . . . a Husband to protect; a Father to provide; a Foundation to support.*

JOHN SPENCER

You're in charge," Bill told his thirteen-year-old son, Barrett, one cold February morning as Bill gave his four children a big hug.

"No, Mom's in charge, but I'll help her," Barrett answered with a smile.

"I'm going to New York City on business, and I'll be back Sunday night. Let's pray together," he said, gathering his kids and wife Pam around him. "I don't want to be late for my plane."

Busy with homeschooling their four children, Pam hardly noticed she didn't get a call from Bill. Three months pregnant with their fifth child, she was relieved to feel better after weeks of nausea and exhaustion. Her husband didn't call as he usually did when he was away. *No worry, he'll be home on Sunday,* Pam thought. Then they'd have a special family dinner to surprise him since they were about to close on their house. What a celebration it was going to be! Even the youngest of their four kids helped get the food and table all ready.

Five o'clock passed. Six o'clock passed. The food got cold, and still Dad wasn't home.

*This is so unlike Bill,* Pam thought. Voted "Most Dependable" in high school, he'd always been the perfect Christian dad and was always on time or called to check in.

*Maybe his plane was delayed.* A call to the airline revealed the plane had landed right on time. Pam waited hours, but he still did not show up. When she contacted the New York hotel where he'd stayed, security discovered his jogging clothes left in the room. She kept calling the hotel, but he wasn't seen again and didn't return for his clothes. Pam stared at the ceiling during a long, sleepless night with worst-case scenarios going through her mind.

The next day the local police department listed Bill as a missing person. Even after a thorough search by a private investigator, no evidence or sign of foul play turned up.

Pam's husband of sixteen years had vanished.

In the course of the next year, Pam and her children struggled with overwhelming grief. She couldn't eat and became a high-risk pregnancy patient. Her fifth child, Harrison, was born six months after her husband's disappearance. Bill left her penniless and in a huge amount of debt he'd never revealed, and she faced the burden of stepping into the workforce. Pam loved her role as a homeschooling mom and homemaker, and losing that to return to the workforce was another blow.

But the most difficult thing she faced was the unanswered questions. *Has Bill been killed? Has some horrible thing happened to him? How will we go on without him?*

A year later Pam and her children saw their father again— not around the dinner table or leading them in prayer but on the television news, wearing handcuffs and surrounded by law enforcement officers. His picture was splashed across state and local newspapers. He had been apprehended in another state, posing under an alias as a widower whose wife and child had died in a car wreck. Although he faced third-degree felony charges for abandoning minor children, Pam requested that the charges be dropped so their family wouldn't be dragged through the courts and media. Bill had no desire to be reunited with his family. He didn't want to see his children. He just wanted a divorce.

As the horror of what had happened sunk in, the sense of overwhelming abandonment, betrayal, and anger would hit Pam in waves. *He lied to me. I'd trusted him with my life. I can't believe this has happened. How can I go on?* Sometimes her emotions immobilized her and she lay in her bedroom, shades and curtains drawn, sobbing.

One day an acquaintance knocked on Pam's door, ignoring the "Please Do Not Disturb" sign.

"She is not seeing visitors," said the visiting neighbor who answered the door.

"I have to talk to Pam," Angie said. Only a few days before Bill left, the two women had met in a bowling alley during a birthday party. Pam knew Angie's husband had left her for another woman and agreed to talk to her.

"How do you seem so together?" Pam asked.

"A pastor from Fort Worth shared some things with me, and the truth set me free," she said.

Pam had no idea what truth Angie was talking about, but Angie sat beside her on the bed. "Today my Bible study teacher thanked God that he has gone before you and behind you and has a course charted for you because he knew you were going to bear this burden."

"God knew about this? God prepared me for this?" On the one hand it was comforting, but on the other, it knocked the wind out of Pam. *Even if I live through this, I don't want to,* she thought. *Why do you declare yourself a loving God and yet planned to drop this in my lap?*

"I know the pastor would make himself available to you if you want to talk," Angie said as she left.

Pam knew she needed someone to help her make sense of her situation, but she had no faith in psychiatrists or psychologists. One had told her she ought to be hospitalized just a few months after her husband had left, but the children had just lost their father. She would not allow them to lose their mother too. A friend had graciously sent her $1,000 to see a renowned psychologist in town, but when she went he asked her the same question over and over, "What happened? What happened?" He didn't offer any real hope and kept looking at his clock as if anxious for the session to be over.

One night Pam went to the Bible study, hoping to talk to this pastor she'd never met. At the close of class, she gathered up her courage and asked if he could meet with her.

They sat down on a bench outside the building, and Pam poured out everything that had happened. "I feel as though I'm dying. I can get dressed in the morning, but I don't have any hope inside of me. If what life holds is poverty and work and all this overwhelming pain, I can't see why I would want to live." Then she waited quietly for the pastor's response.

"First of all, since your husband is gone and I don't know him, he will have to answer to God. But there are two paths you can take: You can keep viewing his sins through a microscope, analyzing them and cataloguing them over and over, or you can say, 'God, although I didn't cause Bill to leave, somewhere I did some things wrong. Open my eyes to see *my sin* and *my weaknesses* and let me deal with those and confess them and praise you that you forgive me from unrighteousness. And then help me deal with forgiving Bill.'

"You see, we fight battles before the Lord in a different way than the world does. We have to recognize that God says he inhabits the praises of his people. If God lives and dwells in the praises of his people, you invite his presence and power into your life and circumstances today through praising him. How's your worship?"

"*Worship?* You don't understand! I am just surviving. I'm *not* in a praise mode."

"If your circumstances have obscured your view of God, then you need to correct that. I want you to read the last seven psalms and let that be your prayer. Think of it as a prescription to take every day. Pray the verses of those psalms aloud to God, because as you declare that this is the truth no matter what the circumstances are, you will encourage your faith," he added.

"I won't feel like it. I can barely lift my voice to sing a hymn in church."

"When you ask your kids to do chores, do you let them disobey if they don't feel like it?" he asked. "'Rejoice always' is a command—God is saying, '*You* rejoice always. *You* pray without ceasing.' It's time to recognize that the Creator of the universe who is being your husband and provider and the father of your children is deserving of your praise. And as you praise him, you will receive a blessing."

This sounded like harsh instructions for a woman so brokenhearted. But the next morning Pam gritted her teeth and said the last seven psalms aloud to God, first in a monotone. It was purely out of obedience, not emotion.

"I will praise you, my God and King, and bless your name forever and ever. I will bless you every day. . . . The LORD is kind and merciful, slow to get angry, full of unfailing love. The LORD is good to everyone. He showers compassion on all his creation" (Ps. 145:1–2, 8–9).

Tears flowed as she continued, "The LORD helps the fallen and lifts up those bent beneath their loads. . . . The LORD is close to all who call on him. . . . he hears their cries for help and rescues them. The Lord protects all those who love him" (Ps. 145:14, 18–20). Gradually reading the psalms aloud to God day after day told her more about God, and she began to feel him lift her up and, against all reason, give her hope.

"Lord, my life really is impossible for me. I am totally impoverished. But I am going to praise you, and I'm going to do the next thing ahead of me," Pam prayed many days as she faced the overwhelming duties of single parenting five children and juggling jobs to make ends meet. She began to see and know God in a new way. He began to show her the majesty of his Word and reveal his truth, that he is a "father to the fatherless" (Ps. 68:5 NASB) and

> Your husband is your Maker,
> Whose name is the LORD of hosts;
> And your Redeemer is the Holy One of Israel,
> Who is called the God of all the earth.
> For the LORD has called you,
> Like a wife forsaken and grieved in spirit,
> Even like a wife of one's youth when she is rejected.
>
> ISAIAH 54:5–6 NASB

She didn't know what it meant that God was a husband to her and a father to her fatherless children, but she asked him to show her and to bridge the gap between her head and heart.

The answer came in small glimpses and moments. One day her twelve-year-old son was playing basketball outside. As she looked at him through the window, she saw him crying and wiping his tears on his shirtsleeve. *He needs his dad, but his dad isn't here. He won't ever be here.* A sense of helplessness washed over Pam as she realized again that she had no way to eradicate the pain of her kids.

Pam asked God, "What do you mean, Lord, that you will be a father to the fatherless?"

"I didn't say I will be. I said, 'I *am* a father to your son.'"

God was saying, "I am," not "I will be" and not "I was," not future tense but *at that moment* and in all the moments a father is needed. Pam thought, *God is my children's father. He* is *my husband*. The light dawned as she got a fresh revelation of her Savior.

Yes, she'd have to accept that truth by faith, because Bill left big shoes to fill. A generous and involved dad, he had biked with his kids instead of playing golf on Saturday. He played with them, did hobbies with them, and was generous with them in meeting their needs. How could anyone fill the gaps he'd left?

Yet as Pam accepted the truth of God's fatherhood by faith, time after time he revealed himself in new ways. A doctor donated thousands of dollars of orthodontic work on her children's teeth. Someone anonymously paid the huge cost of her children's Christian school tuition. Other mothers and fathers helped Pam shoulder the load and nurture her children. Pam's brother, Gill, included the kids on vacations and filled gaps in their lives by going fishing, biking, and playing with them. Joy filled their home so much that people who walked into their house would say, "I love to come into your home. I want my home to be like this."

Nothing changed Pam like the power of God's truth—not the psychologist or the words of well-meaning people who tried to console her. This was true especially in moments that threatened to overwhelm her, such as when the divorce decree was delivered to her. Late that night she felt enveloped in pain as she read the words that divorced Bill from her life forever. The darkness around her pressed in. Life had seemed to unravel, and she was tempted to dwell in the past again, thinking, *What happened? How can I just dismiss sixteen years of my life? How can I possibly move on?*

She pulled her Bible toward her, and her eyes fell on verses she'd underlined long before: "Do not call to mind the former things, or ponder things of the past. Behold, I will do something new, now it will spring forth; will you not be aware of it? I will even make a roadway in the wilderness, rivers in the desert" (Isa. 43:18–19 NASB). Through these verses Pam felt the Lord's compassion and comfort wrapping around her heart and an incredible sense of his love breaking through even when she was preoccupied with her pain.

God has been taking care of Pam and her children for fifteen years. Whenever there is a need, God provides. He is her husband. He is her children's father. It doesn't mean life has been easy or is easy now. But although Pam wouldn't have planned things this way, she is thankful. During trials, she has prayed many times, "Whatever you want me to learn and see of you through this difficulty, show me. Thank you even for the fact that I'm a single mom and have the chance to experience you as husband and father. If you want me to be husbanded by you for my whole life, Lord, I'll be content. You are faithful."

## Catching a Fresh Vision of Jesus

Whether you are single or married, if you have committed your life to Christ, Scripture says that your Redeemer, Jesus, the One who delivered you from the kingdom of darkness into his kingdom of light, is your bridegroom and you are his beloved. It is as if you are at the altar saying, "I do." The Bible contains numerous references to this truth. In Jeremiah 31:32 God refers to himself as the husband of his people. He told them in Hosea 2:16 that in a coming day his people would call him husband instead of master. He promised in Psalm 146 that he would sustain the fatherless and widow. He is forever faithful, and whether we are forsaken by husband, father, or mother and whether we are alone or surrounded by loved ones, Scripture says "the LORD will receive me" (Ps. 27:10 NIV).

*The Psalms prescription.* For a transforming experience in God's Word, take Psalms 144 through 150, as Pam did, and make them your prayer to God morning and night for thirty days. See what new revelations you gain. Don't just read the verses in these psalms. Pray them aloud to God, whether you feel like it or not, as your worship of him. I have found this a sure prescription for depression, anxiety, or feeling overwhelmed. Absorbed over time, God's Word will lift your eyes from the problem to who God is. The power of the Word will change your heart and life.

*Let Scripture bridge the gap between head and heart.* Seeing the Lord as your husband and your children's father may be hard to relate to, so let me encourage you to look up the following verses and meditate on them. As you do, ask the Holy Spirit to bridge the gap between your head and your heart so these truths will sink in:

As a bridegroom rejoices over his bride, so will I rejoice over you.

ISAIAH 62:5 NIV

Your Creator will be your husband. The LORD almighty is his name! He is your Redeemer, the Holy One of Israel, the God of all the earth.

ISAIAH 54:5

"Return home, you wayward children," says the LORD, "for I am your husband."

JEREMIAH 3:14

The LORD . . . cares for the orphans and widows.

PSALM 146:9

Oswald Chambers said, "Jesus appears to those for whom He has done something; but we cannot dictate when He will come. Suddenly at any turn He may come. Now I see Him!"[1] Just as Pam was transformed as she saw Jesus as her husband and her children's father, both in his Word and in real and practical ways in their daily life, so will we be changed as we seek to know and see Jesus as he is.

# Words That Changed a Life

*How glorious a truth it is that when we from our hearts murmur that prayer, "Oh, that someone would get me a drink of water from the well near the gate of Bethlehem," and behold, a tall, cool, crystal-clear glass of water appears before us. Cool and pure and good. This water eases our hot fevered souls and brings life and refreshment to our weary spirits—sick with their wandering, in need of forgiveness and renewal.*

JIM MCGUIGGAN
*JESUS, HERO OF THY SOUL*

The woman wondered if it was safe to approach the well. She studied the man closely. He was fatigued; that much was clear. He had no bucket with him, and he leaned against the rough stones as if the cool exterior might seep through to refresh his weary body. She adjusted the water pot so it wouldn't press into the soft flesh of her shoulders. The man watched her as she walked, but he didn't stare at her like the other men in the city did. She blushed as shame crept from her heart and bled into her cheeks.

She narrowed her eyes, holding back the tears. She would not weep again. The losses in her life had taken away everything she held dear. Five husbands. It was simply too much. Who cared if the women turned aside when she passed them in the street? They hadn't lived her life. They didn't understand the agony of being alone. Perhaps if she could do it over again, she would do things differently, but there was no way to turn back time.

The man stood as she set the water pot on the ground. "Can I have a drink of water?" he asked. He brushed his hand across his dust-streaked brow.

She stared at him, taking in the fine features, considering the inflection of his voice. He was a Jew! It wasn't unheard of for a Jewish man to land in Sychar, but most took extravagant measures to avoid this village. The Samaritans laughed at the pious Pharisees who traveled around the village, adding hard miles to their travel so that they could avoid coming in contact with them. Rabbis would rather be thirsty than violate their religious rules. They weren't allowed to speak to a woman in public, much less a Samaritan woman. It added one more stone to the insults traded between the two races. It was rare for a Jewish man to talk to a Samaritan, but even more surprising that one would request a drink from someone like her.

"Why are you, a Jew, asking me, a Samaritan woman, for a drink?" she asked. She reasoned that his thirst must be greater than his pride under the hot noon sun, but she wanted to hear his answer nonetheless.

The man smiled. "If you knew how generous and gracious God is and who I am, you'd ask me for a drink, and I would give you fresh, living water."

*Why, the man doesn't even have a bucket,* the woman thought. Jacob's well ran deep into the heart of the earth. Did he think he was capable of climbing into the well to draw water from the depths and then carry it to the surface in the palms of his hands?

She asked, "So how are you going to get this 'living water'? Are you a better man than our ancestor Jacob, who dug this well and drank from it, he and his sons and livestock, and passed it down to us?" She turned away to pick up the water pot. The sun had clearly taken its toll on this weary traveler.

"Everyone who drinks this water will get thirsty again and again. Anyone who drinks the water I give will never thirst—not ever. The water I give will be an artesian spring within, gushing fountains of endless life," the man said.

She turned back. Who was this man who spoke with such authority and yet compassion? What was this water he was talking about? She had trudged to the same spot every day since she was old enough to carry the water pot. It was an endless chore. She needed water to drink, to wash the dust from her home, and to bathe. If there were an artesian spring in the area, the word would have spread through the village overnight. Besides, there was no such thing as water that would quench a person's thirst so that they never needed another drink. She had heard enough. Not only was he talking nonsense, but if her neighbors spied her talking to a strange man—a Jew at that—she would endure more gossip.

Dipping the water pot into the well, she let the rope slip gently through her hands. The water seeped into the pot, and she quickly pulled it to the surface, the lean muscles in her arms responding to the familiar task. She poured the cool water into a cup and handed it to the man. He closed his eyes, drinking until every last drop was gone. She picked up the water pot and prepared to leave. The sun was hot and baking her skin, and in the distance she saw a group of people approaching. It was time to go.

Yet she couldn't repress an urge to say, "Sir, give me this water so I won't ever get thirsty, won't ever have to come back to this well again!"

As he stared into her eyes, the woman was gripped by the man's gaze. His voice was gentle but resonated with a quiet, mysterious presence. "Go call your husband and then come back," he said.

"I have no husband," she replied.

"You've had five husbands, and the man you're living with now isn't even your husband. You spoke the truth there," he said. Heat flushed into her face as his words pierced her soul. Water splashed across her robes as she dropped the water pot on the ground. She barely noticed the cold water mixing the dust to mud around her feet, because the secrets of her heart had been revealed.

Had the rumors spread even to Galilee? Surely not! She quickly knelt and sat the water pot upright. This man was like no other man on earth. Perhaps he was a prophet. How else would he know her past? She was angry at herself as the tears pressed against her eyelids. No! She would not cry. She stood and faced him.

"Sir, I perceive you are a prophet! So help me understand this paradox," she begged. She had long desired to know the proper way to approach God. "Our ancestors worshiped God at this mountain, but you Jews insist that Jerusalem is the only place for worship. Which is the right way?"

The man handed her the cup. "The time is coming—it has, in fact, come—when what you're called will not matter and where you go to worship will not matter. It's who you are and the way you live that count before God.

"The true approach to God is in spirit and in truth. God is spirit and he is seeking people who will worship from their hearts, worship based on the truth and through the spirit," the man added.

No one had ever spoken to her with such kindness. It was not just the words but the way he spoke them, as if he knew a secret that she did not. And his voice was so full of compassion. She stood silently, unsure of how to respond. *It does matter what I am called,* she thought. She was a Samaritan, despised by the Jews. She was a woman who was well known because of her association with various men. She was a woman who was judged daily, and she lived under the scrutiny of disapproving looks and sideways glances.

She didn't understand everything this man said, but she wanted to hear more. She had never heard anyone speak the way he did. The prophet—or was he a teacher?—told her wonderful things. He said God was looking for those who were honest, those who would simply be themselves before him in their worship. Perhaps there was a way to have a second chance, even if you had lost your way.

She smiled at the stranger for the first time. "I do know that the Messiah is coming," she said. "When he arrives, we'll get the whole story."

"I am he," the man said. "You don't have to wait any longer or look any further."

She stepped back. Hope ignited small flames that dared to push past the hurt and shame that had branded her. One by one, the walls surrounding her heart began to crumble from the love that emanated from the stranger.

Suddenly she heard footsteps and turned, shying away as several men called out to the man, calling him Jesus. They looked at him and then at her, amazed that he had been speaking with a woman, and a Samaritan woman at that. They didn't say what they were thinking, but their faces showed it (see John 4:27 MESSAGE). This she understood. It was familiar. But then she looked one last time at Jesus, and he smiled directly at her with a look of complete openness and acceptance. She knew without question that this was no ordinary man.

She turned and fled, forgetting the water pot, and made her way to the village. She couldn't wait to tell people about this man who knew about everything she'd ever done, a man who knew her inside and out, knew all the secrets, longings, and pain of her heart, and yet would talk to her and take a drink of water from her hands. He offered her living water and said she'd never thirst again. Maybe he was the Messiah after all![1]

Although the Bible does not name this woman at the well, it does recount how she spread the word about Jesus so enthusiastically that throngs of Samaritans came from surrounding areas to listen to him. They even asked him to stay in their town, and he taught them for two days. Many believed that he was the Messiah and put their faith in him. They told the woman, "We're no longer taking this on your say-so. We've heard it for ourselves and know it for sure. He's the Savior of the world!" (John 4:42 MESSAGE). Four years later when

Philip the Evangelist came to preach in many of the villages of Samaria, he experienced a great gathering of souls, so much so that there was great joy in that city.[2]

## Catching a Fresh Vision of Jesus

We can gain a fresh glimpse of what Christ offered not only to the woman at the well but to each of us when we realize:

*He takes the initiative to seek us,* just as he sought the Samaritan woman. What happened that day at the well? It was a divine appointment. It was a day of transformation. The woman's life—and the lives of scores of people in Samaria—was changed by the living Word of Jesus. He reached out to her and chose to reveal himself to her as the Messiah, something he wasn't doing publicly at that time.

The gesture of asking for a drink might seem small to us, but it transcended several cultural boundaries. This showed that Jesus didn't care about the opinion of others, even his disciples. When they arrived on the scene, they were bewildered. Wasn't this the holy one? Why would he be talking to a Samaritan woman in broad daylight? The well was a common place for people to gather. What if he were seen talking with her?

Yet Jesus was operating on a different level, and his purpose was not an earthly one. Man looks at the outward appearance of things, but God always deals with the heart. His purpose in coming to earth was to bring his light into darkness, to heal that which was broken, and most of all to fling open a door to intimacy with the Father. In the encounter with the woman at the well, Jesus demonstrated this clearly. He offered hope to a woman whose life was in shambles. And he offers hope to you as well, no matter what has occurred in your past. He reaches down to you and pursues you right where you are, a process that can revolutionize your life just as it did this Samaritan woman's.

*In his total forgiveness, he offers a second chance.* He gives a fresh beginning each day. Too often people think that there is no way back when they fail God or others. Many embrace hopelessness when they see the damage they've done to themselves or to their family or friends. It's especially difficult when the sin is public and they are judged by others. This shame can easily become their identity and overshadow the grace that God offers. Yet just as he went out of his way to go by Samaria and meet the woman at the well, Jesus goes out of his way to reach out to those who have lost their way and reveal the truth that the power of his forgiveness is infinitely stronger than any guilt and shame in our lives. You see, the woman at the well had resigned herself to her lot in life, yet God had a greater purpose for her life than she could have imagined. He walked into an area that was off-limits for Jewish men like him to make sure that she had a life-changing encounter.

God is looking for those who will simply be themselves before him. Remember that when we come to him with our mistakes and our sins and ask for a second chance, the living water that Christ described cleanses every sin. Though the woman at the well had a broken past, she began a brand-new future when she gained a fresh vision—not only of Jesus but of who she could be once she drank of the living water that never runs dry. We can do the same.

And once we've seen Jesus and the Savior has left his impression on us, we can't keep it to ourselves. Like the Samaritan woman who told everyone she saw about the Messiah, we will be asking God to open doors for us to tell the story of the one who gave his life so that the living water might spring up in us and spill over to others.

As Oswald Chambers said, "All that God has done for us is the mere threshold; He wants to get us to the place where we will be His witnesses and proclaim Who Jesus is. Be rightly related to God, find your joy there, and out of you will flow rivers of living water."[3]

# FIVE

# A Vision That Endures

*Once it was the blessing,*
*Now it is the Lord;*
*Once it was the feeling,*
*Now it is his Word.*
*Once his gifts I wanted,*
*Now the Giver own;*
*Once I sought for healing,*
*Now himself alone.*

A. B. SIMPSON

Come and see me when you can, darling. I am always ready to entertain my sweet Robert," said the note Hannah found in her husband's coat pocket as she was sorting his clothes on her annual closet-cleaning day. Brokenhearted, she threw the love letter from her husband's mistress into the fire and pondered what had gone so wrong in their marriage. She had suspected from his frequent absences in the evening, but the note confirmed her worst fears. The discovery of her husband's unfaithfulness was devastating, yet Hannah Whitall Smith didn't succumb to despair. Just as she had many other times when waves of tragedy or disappointment rolled over her life, she turned to Christ. That very night she dried her tears and answered a letter from a depressed unmarried friend from England asking how to face the loneliness of her single life. Hannah wrote,

> In my own case, I just determined I would be satisfied with God alone. I gave up seeking after any feeling of satisfaction. I said, "Lord, thou art enough for me, just thyself, without any of thy gifts or blessings. I have thee and I am content. I will be content. I choose to be content. I am content." I said this by faith. I still have to say it by faith often. I have to do so this very evening, for I am not very well and feel what I expect thou would call "low." But it makes no difference how I feel. He is just the same, and He is with me, and I am His, and I am satisfied.[1]

This was not the only time pain had touched Hannah's life. Four of her children died. Her husband suffered several breakdowns and fell into a scandal that brought national humiliation and destroyed his ministry. He left the faith, and his immoral behavior was a consistent thorn in Hannah's flesh. Her three grown children rejected Christianity and embraced the liberal philosophies of the day. One daughter abandoned her husband and children for a lover; the other married one of the boldest atheists of their time. Hannah suffered financial reversals, being shunned by the Quaker family and church she'd been raised in, and family problems. Surely all this would be enough to turn her into a depressed, defeated Christian.

But instead of these trials sinking Hannah's faith and silencing her hopeful writing and preaching, they were a gateway to a closer dependence on God. She remained to the end of her life a faithful wife, mother, and grandmother. She wrote the beloved classic *The Christian's Secret of a Happy Life* and other works which have encouraged the spiritual journey of millions of believers.

How could this woman endure such testings and live an abundant, overcoming life?

Hannah Whitall Smith was sustained by a vision of the steadfast love of Christ—a love awakened in a life-changing revelation many years before. Because of the experience, she knew how to find her joy in this God of all-embracing comfort no matter what happened.

Hannah was a Quaker from birth, born in 1832 into a loving family in Philadelphia, Pennsylvania. Her father, John Whitall, owned a large glass plant in New Jersey, and her mother, Mary, provided an environment where lively Hannah and her three siblings could grow and thrive. Hannah had a happy childhood she described as "one fairy scene of sunshine and flowers."[2] As a teenager she had everything she wished for, and only one thing marred her joy—an aching void in her heart. She knew she wasn't prepared for eternity and didn't feel she ever would be.[3]

A tireless seeker with an adventurous spirit, Hannah wrestled with the conflict between the stern demands of Quaker piety and her desire to experience, learn, and celebrate life and God. She felt herself very rebellious and wanted to be "good," but she never seemed to fit the Quaker mold. At age nineteen she began a new life when she married Robert Pearsall Smith, also a Quaker from birth. They settled in Germantown, Pennsylvania.

While Hannah questioned the beliefs of her Quaker religion, she wanted a closer relationship with a living God. She longed for joy and peace but had not the faintest idea what it meant to "put one's trust in Jesus." In vain she tried to work out her soul's salvation and righteousness based on her own efforts.[4]

In her teens and early twenties she felt in a hopeless spiritual state, cut off from God entirely . . . "like a sinking boat."[5] She grew up believing God was selfishly "intent on His own honor and glory . . . so absorbed in thoughts of Himself and His own righteousness as to have no love or pity to spare for the poor sinners who have offended Him."[6] She wondered why, if God was so good, he would make people who are so bent toward evil. If he was so powerful, why didn't he give people the power to live in the light instead of in darkness? The picture of a stern, harsh God she'd developed in solemn Quaker meetings wasn't a God she could trust or believe in. "A thousand questions rush in on every side," she said. "I am a skeptic!"[7]

This state of unrest and darkness of spirit persisted for over two years. Her Quaker teaching had led to much self-examination and self-absorption. But while she endeavored to muster up inward emotions or a righteous attitude toward God, it only made her religious life miserable. Her soul hungered after God, but she wasn't able to find him.

It was the death of her first child, beloved five-year-old Nellie, that brought a turnaround in her spiritual life. After Nellie died, Hannah struggled not only with grief but with an even more profound sense of distance from God. She couldn't bear the thought that her darling child had "gone out alone into a Godless universe" and yet, no matter where she turned, she found no ray of light.[8]

One day at noon she went out to a religious meeting in one of the busiest parts of the city. As she waited for the speaker to begin, suddenly "an inner eye . . . opened in my soul, and I seemed to see that after all God was a fact—the bottom fact of all facts—and the only thing to do was to find out all about Him."[9]

From that point on, she couldn't rest until she knew him, and she realized that the Bible was the book she needed. When she went to the beach with her family a few weeks later, she took only her Bible and a determination to find God. Sitting in the sand under an umbrella each day, she read the book of Romans, where she discovered that "while we were yet sinners, Christ died for us" (Rom. 5:8 NASB). Here she had her first glimpse of God as he is revealed in the face of Jesus Christ. Her vision of the great unselfishness of God made her "radiantly happy."[10] She now knew without a shadow of a doubt that we were all sinners and therefore all deserved punishment—but Christ had taken our sins upon himself, borne the punishment in our stead, and let us go free. She didn't have to *try* to be righteous or pious. Christ had paid the price and offered her *his* righteousness.

"It was all outside of oneself, and there need be no searching within or rakings up of one's inward feelings to make things right with God," she said.[11] In these moments in the Word, God's extravagant love not only healed and comforted her grief but brought salvation to her soul. She received forgiveness for her sins; "old things passed away" and the new came as she was restored to right relationship with her Savior.[12]

She knew now that God was not a far-off, unapproachable being[13] but a perfect, loving, entirely unselfish God whom she could worship and adore. All her morbid fear of him had vanished. He loved her, he forgave her, and all was right between them.

As a result of this "blaze of illumination,"[14] her desire from that moment on was to live a life abandoned to Christ. The truths in the New Testament became her anchor; all doubting was ended, and her joy became the gladness of knowing Christ as her Redeemer.[15]

Hannah loved nothing better than sharing the truths she'd discovered from the Bible with everyone she met. With this came a terrible burden for the sins of those who were lost and would be separated from God for eternity. How could God possibly bear this? She felt such pain over the desperate, lost people she saw that when she went out on the streets of Philadelphia to events or speaking engagements, she began wearing a heavy dark veil over her face to avoid looking on the faces of sinners. She "imagined these faces lost in hellish fire forever" if they were without Christ.[16]

One day the heaviness was too much to bear, and she cried out to God for "some ray of light, some illumination" on the matter. That afternoon as she traveled across the city on a tram car to speak, her eyes were covered by the veil. But when she looked out of the veil to give the conductor her fare, she glimpsed the worn, sad faces of the two men sitting next to her. Her heart broke for them, and again she silently cried out to God concerning how, being merciful, he could condemn souls like these two men to eternal damnation.

The voice of the Spirit answered, "It is not my will that any should perish but that all should come to eternal life" (see 2

Peter 3:9). For the second time in Hannah's life, a glorious light dawned. God wasn't a selfish God, visiting his love only on some of his creatures. He was love in its very essence. Love was the very law of his being. If she could love her children whether they were bad or good, then God must have something like a mother's love too—only infinitely vast and superior to her own. She also saw that God's love was not just available for a few of his creatures, as was taught in most religious doctrines of her time, but that the sinners she'd met in the street and in the tram car were also God's precious children.[17]

Although Hannah Whitall Smith's concept of universal love was controversial, those early glimpses of Christ's love in the here and now were enough to ravish Hannah's heart and inspire books and messages that have continued to impact millions of people even into the twenty-first century. Her vision of Jesus helped her get a "firm grip on one magnificent foundation truth that nothing has ever been able to shake, and this was that God was in Christ reconciling the world unto Himself . . . the grand central fact of God's love and God's forgiveness."[18] It was a truth on which her soul could rest forever.

## Catching a Fresh Vision of Jesus

Encountering Jesus is a wonderful thing. But sometimes believers' passion for Christ dissipates as trials and tragedies come. We lose our "first love" of Jesus (Rev. 2:4) or become lukewarm (Rev. 3:16). The amazing thing about Hannah Whitall Smith was that she didn't lose her vision of the love of Christ or passion for him even though she endured "troubles and hardships and calamities of every kind" (2 Cor. 6:4). The volumes she wrote contained some of the secrets that kept her vision of Christ alive and led to a happy Christian life—and they have great application for us today. We can experience a fresh vision of Jesus as Hannah did when we:

*Live life on wings.* Hannah Whitall Smith believed that our souls were made to "mount up with wings like eagles" (Isa. 40:31 NASB) and that they could never be satisfied with anything short of flying.[19] We try to break free from the things that frustrate and defeat us by looking for help from outward things like a change of circumstances, marital partners, or financial situations. Yet no earthly refuge can truly give us the deliverance we long for. Instead we are to cast every care upon the Lord and live the life "hidden with Christ in God" (Col. 3:3 NIV) on the "wings of Surrender and Trust."[20] Then, she taught, we are raised into the "clear atmosphere of His presence above our disappointments, thwartings, persecutions, worst enemies, provoking friends, and trials of every sort."[21]

*Focus on the facts instead of feelings.* Our spiritual lives can be revitalized when we do as Hannah did: replace the old, fruitless self-absorption by centering our lives on the glorious Good News declared in the Bible. Hannah persevered with unflinching faith because she believed God's Word and made it her foundation rather than trusting her feelings. She encourages us to base our faith not on emotion but on the nature and character of Christ and his unshakable promises. We no longer fix our thoughts on *How do I feel?* but on *What does God say in his Word?*

*Realize that nothing can separate you from God's love.* Without our trials and hindrances, our wings would be unused and thus wither and lose their flying power, Hannah taught. And yet no matter what happens, no prison or walls on earth can keep us from God.[22] Hannah believed as Paul did that *nothing can separate you from the love of God*. "Death can't, and life can't. The angels can't, and the demons can't. Our fears for today, our worries about tomorrow, and even the powers of hell can't keep God's love away. Whether we are high above the sky or in the deepest ocean, nothing in all creation will ever be able to separate us from the love of God that is revealed in Christ Jesus our Lord" (Rom. 8:38–39 NLT).

Take a deep breath and receive this amazing truth: *Nothing can ever separate you from God's love for you in Christ. Nothing. Ever!* Therefore "God is enough! God is enough for time; God is enough for eternity. GOD IS ENOUGH!"[23]

As we mount up with wings like eagles from our current trial with that kind of assurance, we can praise God in the face of any earthly shaking or problem, for as Hannah said, "the only creature that can sing is the creature that flies."[24]

# PART 2

# A Fresh Vision
## *of* Jesus through
## Service

# SIX

# The Bread *of* Life

*A way of satisfying our brethren's hunger is to share
with them whatever we have.*

MOTHER TERESA

The morning light beamed in my office window as I
pored over my notes for the messages I would give
in Thailand. My husband Holmes and I were leaving
in only a few days, and I had mounds of preparation ahead
of me.

Some of my greatest heroes are missionaries like Amy Carmichael, Lottie Moon, Isabel Kuhn, and Gladys Aylward, and
I am awed by their faith and courage. Now I was to speak
at a retreat for missionaries. *The women coming to this retreat
have years of ministry experience and extensive knowledge of
God and the Bible,* I thought. *What do I have to share with*

*them that they don't already know? I ought to be sitting at their feet as they teach!* The more I labored, the more my sense of inadequacy grew.

*O Lord, help!* I cried.

My thoughts were directed back to the passage from John 6 that I had just been reading:

> Jesus went across the Sea of Galilee (some call it Tiberias). A huge crowd followed him, attracted by the miracles they had seen him do among the sick. When he got to the other side, he climbed a hill and sat down, surrounded by his disciples. It was nearly time for the Feast of Passover, kept annually by the Jews.
>
> When Jesus looked out and saw that a large crowd had arrived, he said to Philip, "Where can we buy bread to feed these people?" He said this to stretch Philip's faith. He already knew what he was going to do.
>
> Philip answered, "Two hundred silver pieces wouldn't be enough to buy bread for each person to get a piece."
>
> One of the disciples—it was Andrew, brother to Simon Peter—said, "There's a little boy here who has five barley loaves and two fish. But that's a drop in the bucket for a crowd like this."
>
> Jesus said, "Make the people sit down." There was a nice carpet of green grass in this place. They sat down, about five thousand of them. Then Jesus took the bread and, having given thanks, gave it to those who were seated. He did the same with the fish. All ate as much as they wanted.
>
> When the people had eaten their fill, he said to his disciples, "Gather the leftovers so nothing is wasted." They went to work and filled twelve large baskets with leftovers from the five barley loaves.
>
> JOHN 6:1–13 MESSAGE

As I read those words, I sensed God saying, "Offer the bread that you have, the messages and words you've written, just like the little boy did. Give it to me, and I will bless it and multiply it to feed all those you are to speak to in Thailand."

So I stacked up the folders of message notes and outlines, offered them up, and earnestly prayed, "Jesus, be very present to take what I bring and distribute and multiply it in the marvelous way only you can throughout each message, each opportunity, and each need we see." I continued preparing my messages but was aware that something had changed. My focus had shifted from *my inadequacy* to *Christ's ability*.

After a twenty-hour flight, we arrived at the Bangkok airport. We spent an hour going through customs and the passport line, directed by people pushing us from place to place while speaking in Thai, which we couldn't understand. Then we searched and searched for the Irish pastor who was supposed to pick us up. It was after midnight, and we were exhausted as we combed the sea of faces.

Finally I went up to an American-looking couple and asked if they were our ride. They weren't, but they called the Overseas Missionary Fellowship office and were told that the man scheduled to pick us up wasn't coming, so we were to take a taxi to a hotel and come back to the airport in the morning to catch our flight for Chiang Mai.

I was irritated and tired, inwardly grumbling that things had gone awry on our first night. My "bread" seemed to be shrinking already. But on the little plane north to Chiang Mai, I was encouraged by the verses in my morning reading: "God is able to make all grace abound to you, so that in all things at all times, having all that you need, you will abound in every good work" (2 Cor. 9:8 NIV) and "This service you perform is not only supplying the needs of God's people but is also overflowing in many expressions of thanks to God" (2 Cor. 9:12 NIV).

We arrived in hot, humid Chiang Mai to the smiles and warm welcome of Larry and Paula Dinkins and Judy Clark, the pastor's wife, who held bouquets of beautiful flowers. It was the rainy season, but even when it wasn't raining, Holmes and I looked as if we'd been in a rain shower because we broke out in sweat as soon as we stepped outside into the heat.

On the way up the mountain to the retreat location, we stopped at Agape House, an HIV/AIDS orphanage, to pray for the babies and young children. We saw God's grace in abundance in the bright eyes of the children and the sacrificial giving of the volunteers.

That weekend I spoke to women from Sweden, Zimbabwe, Ireland, Australia, England, America, France, Switzerland, Germany, Burma, India, Thailand, New Zealand, and other countries. They were dedicated missionaries from OMF, Pioneers, Vista Pacific, Wycliffe, and other organizations.

At the last moment before a message, a different story would come to my mind, a little change in direction or a Scripture I hadn't considered. New bread! That weekend I discovered that missionaries are just like you and me: they become broken or weary, in need of Christ's bread and his refreshment to their souls.

I woke at 6:00 A.M. on Sunday violently ill with an intestinal bacteria. Cramping, a high fever, and a severe headache flattened me. I somehow dragged myself to the last worship time and then got in the car for the trip to the city, where that night I was to speak for two hours at Chiang Mai International Church's evening services.

How I got up to speak for two services back-to-back as sick as I was is still a mystery to me, but although I felt very ill, God gave me grace and strength the moment I got up from my chair, and he passed out much "bread."

Tuesday morning Paula Dinkins, the missionary hosting us, drove me to speak to a group of Thai mothers who were Christians. My heart was moved by seeing that mothers' hearts are universally burdened for their children, and these women were so eager to hear how to pray for their sons and daughters. These Thai mothers were desperately worried about their children getting a good education and anxious about their kids' bad friends, materialism, and drugs. They soaked up every Scripture and word of hope I offered, and then we all prayed together for their children.

That evening a large group of Chinese-Thai men and women gathered—professors, doctors, a lawyer, a publisher, and other professionals—and I spoke with the assistance of a brilliant translator. These intellectuals were intense about wanting to help their children succeed and grow as Christians. After several more days of meetings and speaking, I remarked to Holmes, "Honey, I'm all finished, at least with the big gatherings," and breathed a sigh of relief.

However, right after we returned from the evening event I'd spoken at, the phone rang. It was Avis, the director of the Agape House orphanage. Little Mac, a five-month-old baby we'd prayed for the weekend before, had died. Avis asked me to speak at his funeral.

*Lord, I've never spoken at a funeral service,* I silently prayed. *There are plenty of ministers here who could do a better job.*

Paula urged me to say yes. "This is a *great* ministry opportunity," she said. As missionaries who'd been in the field for over twenty-one years, Paula and Larry saw everything in their path as a ministry opportunity and would not hear of my not accepting this one.

When I finally fell asleep that night, the words to share still hadn't come. But in the middle of the night, I was awakened and slipped to my knees to pray in the dark as rain pelted on the roof. Suddenly the words God wanted me to share at Mac's service flowed into my mind and onto paper.

When we walked into the orphanage the next morning, a crowd of visitors and Agape House volunteers stood solemnly around a baby crib. On a delicate, pale blue quilt lay the body of the baby we had prayed for last Friday—little Mac, all dressed up in a precious embroidered white outfit and baby socks. Above his head in the crib was a basket of the most beautiful long-stemmed pink roses I had ever seen.

After we all sang "How Great Thou Art" and "In His Time," I spoke, with Avis's husband translating. Then we sang hymns as each person took a pink rose from another basket and one by one carefully laid them on Mac's body. The hot, humid room was filled with the sound of weeping and the voices of the babies and preschool children the volunteers and nannies had sitting on their laps. The children also laid their pink roses in the baby's crib.

Not until after the service was I told that the group of eight volunteers who had just arrived from Holland were not believers. Then I understood why the Holy Spirit had given me such a clear presentation of the gospel to share. Once again Jesus had distributed bread.

Since I was beginning to think a little more like a missionary, I wasn't quite as surprised when another "ministry opportunity" presented itself late that Thursday afternoon.

The wife of the police chief of Chiang Mai asked me to come to a luncheon at her home the next day. She had invited her Buddhist friends and wanted me to speak to them in a private presentation on a topic of her choosing. The problem was that she didn't tell me in advance what topic she was choosing!

*Lord, what do you have in mind? Prepare my heart and help me to rest in you and listen to you,* I prayed that night.

The next day I was driven to a very elegant, large home, a place much more lavish than any other we'd seen in Thailand, to a "going away luncheon" planned by Tuk, the police chief's wife. In Thailand the police chief of a city is as important as the mayor. Gathered around the table were Thai women from the American consulate and the consul general's office.

After a sumptuous lunch, Tuk said, "Tell us how our children can become successful in school; share with us about being a good parent." I had no notes, but God provided the words to speak to these women for almost an hour. Though staunchly Buddhist, the women so desired successful children that their hearts were willing to listen to a Christian from America share new ideas and concepts with them.

After the luncheon I led a three-hour writing workshop for homeschool parents and kids and hardly had time to take a breath before Holmes and I were driven to the Chiang Mai airport for the long return journey home. As I leaned my head back in the airplane seat, I thought of all the times bread had been distributed—and who was the source of it all.

I recalled that one day when Jesus was teaching, a crowd of Jewish people said that Moses gave their ancestors bread from heaven to eat in the wilderness, and they challenged Jesus to show them a miraculous sign. But Jesus knew the real source of the bread the Israelites had received on their sojourn out of Egypt. He said, "I assure you, Moses didn't give them bread from heaven. My Father did" (John 6:32). So it was in Thailand. The Bread of Life had shown up and fed many people.

I had seen the same Jesus who said, "I am the bread of life. No one who comes to me will ever be hungry again" (John 6:35). This fresh vision of Jesus as the Bread of Life changed my perspective on speaking, serving, and ministry. It was a lesson not just for that trip but for a lifetime. Now whenever I am asked to speak or serve, whether close to home or hundreds of miles away, I know that I am to give all that I am to Jesus and simply bring the bread he's given me, asking and trusting that he will bless it, multiply it, and give it to meet the needs of each heart. And he never fails!

## Catching a Fresh Vision of Jesus

When we serve others, share the gospel, or offer hope and help, we get a chance to join Jesus in what he is doing—drawing people to himself and extending his kingdom. Here are some ways to experience and see Jesus in your everyday life.

*Seize ministry opportunities wherever you find them.* Look at unexpected happenings and interruptions to your schedule as invitations to serve. When we respond with a servant's heart and offer the Lord all we have and are, he can take our little offering and multiply it. As my friend Fern Nichols told me once, "We do the small obedience and God does the grand thing."

Whether it is serving the poor, speaking, teaching a group of kids, leading a women's ministry, loving your neighbor or family, or working in your vocation, remember who your source of life is and point people to *him*. Give God the credit as people are blessed. It's all his plan; he simply lets us partner with him in doing our part. Jesus said, "This is what my Father wants: that anyone who sees the Son and trusts who he is and what he does and then aligns with him will enter real life, eternal life. My part is to put them on their feet alive and whole at the completion of time" (John 6:40 MESSAGE). Ask the Lord, "What's my part?"

*Work while resting and trust the results to God.* Jesus said, "Don't waste your energy striving for perishable food. . . . Work for the food that sticks with you, food that nourishes your lasting life, food the Son of Man provides. He and what he does are guaranteed by God the Father to last" (John 6:27 MESSAGE). Striving is doing things in our own strength, worrying about pleasing people with our performance. Working while resting, on the other hand, is doing our preparation and yielding to God, then letting him do the work through us. And as we work by resting rather than striving, we will see Jesus more and more because he will be the one doing more than we could ask or imagine (see Eph. 3:20–21).

Much of the striving we do in life doesn't produce lasting results anyway. But what the Lord Jesus does through us, that bread we offer from him, nourishes the "lasting life" of others, and we gain a clearer vision of the Savior. With our confidence and focus upon him, we can simply do our part and trust the results to God. And as we invite Christ to use us, great things can happen. God is always doing great things, whether or not we take time to notice them!

# SEVEN

# The Face *of* Jesus

*The greatest form of praise is the sound of consecrated
feet seeking out the lost and helpless.*

BILLY GRAHAM

Richard Drake strained his eyes as he looked at the cancer cell cultures under the microscope in his laboratory. As usual, some of the experimental treatments were working and others were not. In spite of the importance of his studies, his mind kept drifting back to the congregational meeting the previous day. He felt a sharp contrast between the preciseness of his work in the lab and the messiness of dealing with people and church problems.

The meeting had dragged on for hours with discussion of a new construction plan, church direction, and accusations about the minister. Church politics was Richard's least favorite part of Christianity, and he had seen some of the worst in people he'd thought were such good Christians. In fact, there were lots of things hard to swallow about organized religion. *Where's God in all this anyway?* he wondered. *Why am I even involved with these hassles?*

His mind drifted into critical questioning mode as it sometimes did at church—until the vivid memory of an experience he'd had one winter several years before interrupted his thoughts.

In 1993 Richard had been researching treatments for HIV, the virus that causes AIDS. Progress was slow, and new treatment strategies that later proved effective didn't emerge until 1996. All the knowledge Richard had gained about HIV was from research journals and sterile laboratory experience, and he began to realize he'd never seen the human side of the disease. Wanting to help in a more personal way, he joined a seven-member RAIN (Regional AIDS Interfaith Network) care team to provide help to local people with AIDS who'd been shunned by their families and the community. Destitute and dying, they were in desperate need of help. The RAIN teams provided meals, transportation to doctor's appointments, hospital visits, and whatever else was necessary to meet their needs.

John was the first care partner Richard's team had contact with, and he was a difficult man to help. He was depressed and alienated from his family. Many of his friends had died from the disease. Lonely and belligerent, John sometimes let his anger spill out onto the team. But Richard had learned from his RAIN training not to look for any reward or blessing for himself in the ministry, so John's oppositional personality wasn't a problem. In fact, Richard grew to like John, and the team members did whatever they could to help him.

After Christmas John became critically ill with pneumonia. For two weeks he was in and out of the hospital, but surprisingly he rallied enough to go home. However, his health continued to spiral downward, and with no more insurance and a bank account drained by hospitalizations, he soon had to be moved to a friend's place.

The RAIN team volunteered to help John clean out his apartment. John lay on the couch, so weak all he could do was watch as the team cleaned, packed, and moved his furniture out. Though he was once a strong, independent man, his body was wasting away. Richard wished John would be his feisty old self, but he didn't seem to have the energy to even speak.

Finally everything in the apartment had been moved out except the couch John was lying on. Since he didn't have the strength to walk to the car, the team wrapped him in blankets, creating a makeshift gurney. Each of the four volunteers held a corner of the blanket, with Richard holding the front right side by John's chest. He was cocooned inside with his arms folded across his chest as the team lifted him up and headed out the door to the stairs.

Richard was amazed at how heavy John seemed, and he and the other team members strained and sweated as they went down the steps as carefully as possible so as not to jar John. However, as they carried him around the side of the apartment building halfway to the car, they slipped on an icy patch and almost lost their grip on him. While they tried to stabilize their hold on John, Richard suddenly felt as if he was seeing everything in slow motion. Background noises faded out and everything seemed silent, still, and surreal.

As he looked down, something incredible happened. Both of John's bony arms had flailed out of the blanket, but his legs were still bound together like he was on a crucifix. Then John looked up at Richard with an expression that will be forever imbedded in his memory. It was not a look of pain or fear but of total peace and love, something Richard had never before seen on anyone's face.

Suddenly it didn't look like John anymore. Richard saw another man's face. *What in the world just happened?* he thought. Seconds later, the team regained control. Everything sped up to normal pace; the noises flooded in again. They walked the rest of the way down the hill with John enfolded in the blankets and loaded him safely in the back of a station wagon.

When they arrived at the friend's place, they carried John in. As they laid him down, Richard noticed a framed picture of Christ over the bed. *Not entirely a coincidence,* he thought. Early the next day, John's friend took him back to the hospital, where John died that evening.

Richard couldn't get the image he'd seen when he looked in John's face out of his mind. It kept bugging him, and no amount of analyzing seemed to help. *Was it just the intensity and stress of moving John?* his scientist's mind wondered. *Is there a biochemical explanation for what I saw?*

At John's memorial service, Richard began telling his minister about what had happened. The minister had also been one of the four team members carrying John to the car and had been on the front left side of John. He interrupted Richard before he finished his description. "I know what you mean, Richard. I saw it too. The face of Christ."

That was just what Richard had seen looking back at him from the makeshift gurney that held John's dying body: the face of Jesus. He saw a glimpse of Christ in the face of that dying man and knew it was the face of all those who suffer.

The RAIN team cared for other people with AIDS. Each person was different. But Richard never forgot John and the image he'd seen while caring for him.

Like the disciple Thomas, Richard tends to question and doubt. As a scientist who seeks to unlock the mysteries of our biological systems, he finds it hard to turn off critical analysis when he goes to church. But whether he's questioning doctrine, frustrated with petty quarrels and power struggles on church committees, or disillusioned with a minister who has fallen into sin, the vision he saw that winter day grounds him, draws him back to God, and somehow renews his faith. It reassures him that our Lord is truly alive and comes to us in many different ways.

Richard hadn't gone looking for a blessing in serving someone who was suffering. But what he experienced had a profound personal impact. Through the years he's drawn on the encouragement he gained from that glimpse into the unseen that the Lord gave him.

We shouldn't be surprised that we can encounter the Lord while serving a sick or suffering person. Jesus said,

> "I was hungry, and you fed me. I was thirsty, and you gave me a drink. I was a stranger, and you invited me into your home. I was naked, and you gave me clothing. I was sick, and you cared for me. I was in prison, and you visited me."

Then these righteous ones will reply, "Lord, when did we ever see you hungry and feed you? Or thirsty and give you something to drink? Or a stranger and show you hospitality? Or naked and give you clothing? When did we ever see you sick or in prison, and visit you?" And the King will tell them, "I assure you, when you did it to one of the least of these my brothers and sisters, *you were doing it to me!*"

MATTHEW 25:35–40 (emphasis added)

When we serve those in need, the "least" in the world's eyes, we often receive the unexpected blessing of seeing the face of Jesus in them.

## Catching a Fresh Vision of Jesus

How do you and I get a new glimpse of Jesus? Mother Teresa said Jesus is who we serve in the poor, so as we get closer to them, we get closer to Christ.[1] Richard and his team started by reaching out to only one man, and their efforts may seem like a drop in the bucket compared to the worldwide problem of AIDS. Mother Teresa felt the same way. "I picked up one person," she said. "Maybe if I didn't pick up that one person I wouldn't have picked up the others. The whole work is only a drop in the ocean. But if we don't put the drop in, the ocean would be one drop less. Same thing for you . . . just begin . . . one by one."[2]

Here are some ways we can begin to get a fresh vision of Jesus through serving others one by one, especially the "least of these":

*Take care of those at home and ask God to expand your heart.* Mother Teresa said, "Love begins by taking care of the closest ones—the ones at home. Let us ask ourselves if we are aware that maybe our husband, our wife, our children, or our parents live isolated from others, do not feel loved enough, even though they may live with us."[3]

As you love those close to you, ask the Lord to expand your heart beyond the borders of your own family and fill it with his love for the broken and needy. Don't neglect to look around to those who are sick, those who are battling addictions, and those who are poor or lonely that you could care for, befriend, or join with others to minister to. In doing the work of Jesus we experience him in new ways as we allow him to love others through us. You could ask God to make you willing with a prayer like, "Lord, let me be your hands and feet. Show me what's on your heart for those around me, and give me a servant's heart, a surrendered heart, and eyes to see people the way you see them."

*Be open to new ways the Lord Jesus may reveal himself to you.* In J. B. Phillips's classic *Your God Is Too Small*, he said, "We can never have too big a conception of God, and the more scientific knowledge . . . advances, the greater becomes our idea of His vast and complicated wisdom."[4] Our spiritual lives are hindered by putting God in a box and only expecting to experience him in church or in an activity designed to nurture our own souls.

We may expect to sense his presence when we are listening to an inspiring worship CD, at a special conference, or at an extravagant Christian concert. But Kay, an artist I know, sees Jesus in the faces of children who are battling cancer. As she helps these kids create art projects to take their minds off painful treatments, she encounters God in amazing and unforgettable ways. My friend Tony, who volunteers at a daily breakfast for homeless people, encounters Jesus again and again as he serves pancakes and sausage and gives food baskets away. Mary Ann, another friend, sees glimpses of the love of Christ in foster mothers she works with in ChildShare, a ministry to provide homes for neglected children.

What unexpected places might you see Jesus in your world? What do you see in your community or the world that breaks your heart or that you can't stop thinking about? Perhaps you see it while working with children. Jesus put a little child in his arms and said, "Anyone who welcomes a little child like this on my behalf welcomes me" (Mark 9:37). Perhaps you see it on a mission trip or in a nursing home. Whatever it is, consider whether it could be a key to where God may be leading you to serve others and in the process see anew the King of Kings, who took up a towel to serve his disciples and poured out his life that we—and the whole world—might not perish but have eternal life.

# EIGHT

# An Expectant Heart

*Those who keep speaking about the sun while walking under a cloudy sky are messengers of hope, the true saints of our day.*

HENRI J. NOUWEN

S imeon willed his aged legs to carry him quickly to the temple courts. A sense of urgency consumed him. He nodded in respect to those who called out his name, but he didn't stop to pass the time of day. Today was an important day, although he wasn't sure why or what lay ahead. He recognized the powerful but tender nudging of the Holy

Spirit. He must be present in the temple courts, and he hastened to obey that calling (see Luke 2:27).

When Simeon arrived, he bent to catch his breath. Once his heart slowed down, he stood and gazed at the temple. He felt so at home in this place where he had spent his life studying the Law and serving God. He loved to share the stories of the great deeds of Jehovah and the rich history of the Jewish faith with the younger ones who clamored to hear him. He was a prophet, a man of God, and the temple was his sanctuary—not a mere building, but a consecrated place. This was where he could give back to God what he had so generously been given. This was where he worshiped day after day. Many listened when he spoke, but Simeon did not seek their approval. His only desire was to please and serve God.

As he climbed the steps, the catch in his chest deepened. Simeon knew that he was in the final stages of his life. He was far along in years, and his body was weary. All that remained before he went on to his eternal reward was the fulfillment of a promise. Years ago the Holy Spirit had revealed to Simeon that he would not die until he had seen the Messiah (see Luke 2:26).

A breeze pushed his robes against his ankles. Perhaps it would be a day like today when he saw the King of Kings. Would the Messiah wear a crown? Would he be a warrior with great courage to lead his people to victory?

His thoughts were interrupted when the gate opened and a couple entered the courtyard. The man was dressed like a laborer, a craftsman. He clutched a crude cage in his hands, with two pigeons inside pushing against one another as he walked. His young wife walked close by his side, a baby snuggled in her arms. Simeon nodded. Today must be the fortieth day after the birth of the child. According to the Law, two pigeons or two doves would suffice for the purification offering when a family could not afford a lamb.

As the mother glanced his way and their eyes met, something in Simeon's soul quickened. He held out his arms, and the mother tenderly handed him the babe. Simeon gazed at the child. Suddenly years of intellectual understanding were replaced by a sense of awe as he looked into the face of the infant. He wasn't sure how, but every fiber of his being confirmed what his heart told him. He had studied about him, spoken to others about his coming, and encouraged fellow Jews to put their hope in him. But now, as he looked into the eyes of the child, the truth burst through his soul.

This was the Messiah!

A tiny babe! How could it be? "Where was he born?" Simeon asked.

"Bethlehem," the father replied solemnly.

"Bethlehem!" Just as Isaiah had prophesied! Simeon lifted the baby in the air and praise erupted from the depths of his soul. His joy overflowed like a spring of sweet water as he sang,

> Sovereign Lord, as you have promised,
> you now dismiss your servant in peace.
> For my eyes have seen your salvation,
>     which you have prepared in the sight of all people,
> a light for revelation to the Gentiles
> and for glory to your people Israel.
>
> LUKE 2:29–32 NIV

Simeon rejoiced before God as if he were a man reborn. He nestled the child against his chest and stood before the young couple. The mother's cheeks were damp as she smiled through her tears. The father's face shone with humility at the words spoken by the prophet (see Luke 2:33). Simeon reached out and blessed the young family, his heart full of happiness yet heavy as the reality of the Scriptures imprinted in his mind became clear.

He placed the child back in the mother's arms, saying, "This child is destined to cause the falling and rising of many in Israel" (Luke 2:34 NIV). He sadly shared the hard truth of the future of the Promised One: "And a sword will pierce your own soul too" (Luke 2:35 NIV). The couple solemnly nodded as if the words revealed what they already knew in their hearts.

Not far away, the sounds of a faithful widow worshiping God filled the air. She had risen from her knees to stand and watch Simeon as he rejoiced with the child in his arms, but her praises continued to flow. "This is Anna," Simeon told the couple. "She is a prophetess, a righteous woman."

Anna's husband had died young, and she had been a widow most of her eighty-four years. She could have withdrawn from God in her grief when "death ravaged her home," but "she did not bury her hope in a grave. In place of what God took, He gave her more of Himself. She became devoted to Him who had promised to be as a Husband to the widow and in her long widowhood was unwearying in her worship."[1]

Anna had devoted her life to praying for others, crying out day and night unto God. She was thin, for she fasted continually.[2] Seeing Anna kneeling in worship and prayer in the temple court was as familiar as seeing the sun shine each morning.

She hesitated for a moment, then walked toward Simeon. "Could it be?" she asked. Her weathered face gazed at the child, hope in her eyes. Like Simeon's, Anna's mind was saturated with Old Testament prophecies and promises concerning the coming of the "seed of the woman to bruise the serpent's head."[3]

Simeon nodded. "Yes, Anna, it has come to pass," he said. "The Messiah is here!"

After gazing upon the face of the Christ child and basking in the goodness of God for a few precious moments, she turned and ran. Her back was bent with age, but her steps were quick as she spilled the news to those who had gathered around the courtyard.

"The redemption of Israel has arrived!" she called out. "The Messiah has come!" Though her eyes were failing from age, they shone brightly from those few moments of seeing Jesus, and tears of joy slipped down her cheeks.

These two godly servants, Simeon and Anna, played no great role on the stage of Bible history. Some might even call them "bit" players, yet God chose them to be witnesses. They were chosen to confirm what had been spoken generations before. It was no accident that they were in the right place at the right time. They were expecting God, and when he called, they heard his voice.

Simeon's and Anna's hearts were fixed on something they could not see. Their attitudes were that of worshipers as they waited for God's timing. Until the moment Simeon saw the baby Jesus, he lived by faith alone. His mind had long been brimming with knowledge about the Chosen One, but seeing Jesus in the flesh was the fulfillment of all that he had believed and hoped for. The joy he expressed as he sang praises in the temple court was that of a man who had seen a promise fulfilled right before his eyes. Simeon was so satisfied with his vision of Jesus that he experienced total peace. One look had given him all he needed to move on to his heavenly reward.

Anna too had lived a life of faithful service and devotion. Widowed in her youth, she had been left "desolate" and perhaps had faced a "long, lonely, and cheerless" existence.[4] Yet she gave her all to God, going to the temple faithfully each day after mundane day and year after year to pray for the coming of the Messiah. When the miracle occurred and he was brought to the temple by his mother and father, Anna's faith, like Simeon's, was rewarded.

## Catching a Fresh Vision of Jesus

Have you ever served God faithfully while waiting for his promises to come to pass yet seen only delays? Have you experienced how "hope deferred makes the heart sick" (Prov. 13:12 NIV)? Sometimes it's hard to hold fast when daily circumstances contradict God's promises. Simeon and Anna were able to wait with hope because they fixed their eyes on God alone. Since they were both elderly and the promise was a long time in coming, they could have become disappointed in God and dismissed the nudge of the Holy Spirit when the young couple arrived in the temple court.

The king whom Simeon and Anna expected was a warrior, not a baby. By all appearances the couple that came into the temple that day was poor. But because Simeon and Anna lived a life of expectancy, they recognized the unlikely answers that only God could have delivered. We too can see God's promises fulfilled if we:

*Live expectantly, tuned in to the Spirit.* When we pattern our lives to seek God, we learn to recognize the voice of the Holy Spirit. We become sensitive to that prompting and are available when God calls us to witness his handiwork. We can find comfort when we are tired or impatient to see those promises take place. The Holy Spirit can show us things that others might not see or understand, just like the promise to Simeon that he would see the Messiah before he died. But we are unlikely to hear the Spirit's voice unless we prepare ourselves to do so by seeking God. The Lord becomes real and our hearts become expectant as God provides a fresh vision of himself in our quiet times with him. Just like he did for Simeon and Anna, God will kindle the joy in your soul when knowledge about him is transformed into relationship with him. It can be like seeing him for the very first time.

When we eagerly look for God, we may find him in unexpected moments and even places we've been hundreds of times. The Bible shares many promises for our daily lives, but we can also look forward to the eternal promise he gave each of us: *He is coming again.* That's a great hope. Just as the Holy Spirit promised Simeon that the Messiah would come, we have been promised that our Savior will come again for those who are looking for him.

Let us be among those who say, "Behold, this is our God; we have waited for Him, and He will save us. This is the Lord; we have waited for Him; we will be glad and rejoice in His salvation" (Isa. 25:9 NKJV).

Expectancy. It's an attitude of the heart.

*Be a missionary.* Anna not only expected good things from God but shared that hope with others around her when the promise came to pass. Bursting with joy, she didn't keep the incredible news to herself. In fact, Anna became "the first female herald of the Incarnation to all who looked for the Redeemer in Jerusalem," a true missionary.[5] We too have the opportunity to share the promise with those around us. And though some are called to other nations, you don't have to leave the country to share God's Good News.

If you have encountered Christ, talk about his salvation and glory with others you meet, as Anna and Simeon did. When you get up each day, say, "Lord, put in my path those who are looking for you and want to know you, prodigals who have strayed away and lost sheep who need you. Help me to see my company as a mission field or my school as a place full of people with a God-shaped vacuum inside. Give me your gentle words to share the hope that is within me!" As we intercede for others and speak of the reality of Christ, perhaps we will be the witnesses when one of our loved ones or friends have the opportunity to look into the face of the Savior and see a vision of him themselves for the very first time.

# NINE

# Jehovah
# Is Still God

*Oh, the fullness, pleasure, sheer excitement of knowing
God on Earth!*

JIM ELLIOT

No matter how long we've been Christians, we all need a fresh revelation of Jesus. At some point each of us will encounter circumstances so overwhelming or storms so difficult that we will lose our perspective and need to lift our eyes from the turmoil on earth to the truth of who God is.

In the first scene of the movie *The Inn of the Sixth Happiness*,[1] a dowdy woman in a worn blue coat and hat gets off a train in London carrying only a brown suitcase and purse and begins searching for the office of the China Missionary Society.

"You *are* going to send me to China, aren't you? You are going to use me, aren't you?" she asks the director.

"You're just not qualified," he tells her. "Our missionaries are specially trained in languages and well-educated, and you . . ."

It wasn't the first nor would it be the last time she heard "you're not qualified." No matter that the actress Ingrid Bergman was much taller than the frail, five-foot Gladys Aylward or that Ingrid had light brown hair while Gladys's hair was black. The actress portrayed well the terrible disappointment Gladys felt at being turned down for the only thing she desired to be: a missionary to China.

"God, here's my Bible! Here's my money! Here's me! Use me, God!" Gladys cried after the heartbreaking rejection. Now it seemed that every door had closed. She had tried for years to be a missionary, but the only jobs she could get were as a nanny and a parlor maid. She had prepared for the mission field by practicing making speeches in London's Hyde Park; she had ministered to the poor in the slums of Bristol and served as a Rescue Sister in South Wales. She studied hard at the China Inland Mission school, but her scores weren't high enough for her to be accepted into that or any other mission society. All she heard was, "You're too old to learn the Chinese language. Your education is inadequate. Why, you've only worked as a servant. Your health isn't good enough."

She might have been discouraged, but the plucky British woman was not deterred from her goal. Taking a position as a housemaid for two retired missionaries, Gladys saved her shillings for the cheapest transportation to China because she had heard that an elderly missionary needed help. The grueling journey would take her across the English channel by boat and then by train through Holland, Germany, Poland, and Russia and finally to China.

The hardships Gladys encountered on the long trip would have made a strong man turn back. She endured weeks of rugged train travel and two days and nights of walking in deep snow in frigid temperatures, almost freezing to death. She spent cold, hungry nights on train station platforms in Siberia; she was interrogated and her passport was confiscated. Dreadfully ill, she had to take a detour on a Japanese ship to get to China and then take two arduous train journeys and several teeth-rattling bus rides before arriving in Tsehchow—only to find that the woman she was coming to assist wasn't even there.[2]

Finally, after traveling on mule trains through wild, rugged territory controlled by warlords, Gladys reached the remote mountain village of YangCheng, where she met the elderly missionary, Mrs. Jeannie Lawson, she had come to serve. Together they prepared "The Inn of Eight Happinesses," an evangelistic outreach to mule train drivers. They hoped the muleteers would in turn carry the gospel message hundreds of miles through China.

"You just feel where you belong as if you were told. For me it's China," Gladys once said while still in London. China did become her home, and the native dress of blue jacket and trousers became her daily garb. Soon she was telling Bible stories to muleteers, helping Mrs. Lawson run the inn, and ministering to people in mountain villages. However, within a year of Gladys's arrival, Jeannie Lawson died. Gladys was left with The Inn of the Eight Happinesses to run, mission work to do in the villages, no money, and overdue taxes to pay on the inn.

She talked to God about these problems, and God answered by providing a miraculous opportunity: the mandarin, the highest authority in the territory, wanted Gladys to be his employee. She became the official foot inspector of the province of Shansi, with the job of unbinding the feet of every young girl. In this important position, Ai-weh-deh, "the virtuous one," or small woman, as she was called by the people because of her size, could tell Bible stories and share about the love of Jesus wherever she went. While unbinding feet throughout the towns, villages, and caves of the mountains, she freed the minds and hearts of the Chinese people to know and love God.

As time passed, Gladys made scores of converts, and her influence grew. Even the mandarin became her close friend and admired her wisdom and strength. She became a Chinese citizen in 1936 and spoke Chinese dialects as fluently as a native. Years of happy, productive ministry flew by for Gladys.[3]

Yet this woman who had defied the odds, survived horrific challenges, converted villages, and even single-handedly stopped a violent riot in the YangCheng prison came to a desperate moment in which she faced a mission so impossible that she wondered where God was.

It happened when Japan invaded China and began slaughtering its people. At the same time China's nationalist and communist armies were engaged in civil war. Gladys's town, YangCheng, was not exempt from the violence. Gladys, their cook Yang, and Gladys's adopted children were praying upstairs when the inn and other parts of the town were bombed from airplanes.[4] Gladys was rescued from the rubble, bruised and sick, yet aided the wounded in YangCheng.

One day Gladys returned to YangCheng from the mission station in Tsehchow to find the dead bodies of scores of men, women, and children who had been shot or run through with bayonets by Japanese troops. The streets ran with blood; parents and orphaned children wailed in grief. With the enemy advancing again, Gladys took her own adopted children and the orphaned little ones of YangCheng up to the highest village in the mountains and took care of them. After being shot in the back by Japanese soldiers who had pursued them into the hills, Gladys had to leave the province with her adopted children and one hundred children who had been orphaned by the massacre. Their goal was to reach safety across the mountains in free China.

The journey out of war-torn YangCheng to an orphanage in free China was dangerous. Bone-weary and injured, Gladys became ill on the journey. She and the children had little food and had to scavenge in villages along the way. Sleeping in the open, they were soaked when it rained and thirsty and hungry much of the time. The children cried in misery from blistered, swollen feet. Gladys led them in singing hymns to keep them going on the trek of miles and miles over the mountains.

After one long, sleepless night, Gladys saw no hope of going on. Before her was the 2,600-mile-long Yellow River. The river was closed to crossing boats; she had no way to get the children across. At that point, Gladys felt like giving up. She knew she couldn't walk on water and saw absolutely no way they could go any farther.

Listening through the night to the distant rifle fire signaling the approach of the enemy, Gladys heard the orphans whimper in hunger as they lay on the ground. The last crumbs of food were gone. She struggled with despair as never before in her life. *What will become of the children?* she thought. *Will Japanese soldiers come and kill us all? Will we starve? Has this journey been a terrible mistake?*

The next morning Sualan, a thirteen-year-old girl, reminded Gladys of a story she had told them many times—the story of Moses and of how God parted the Red Sea so the Israelites could cross it.

"Why does God not open the waters of the Yellow River for us to cross?" Sualan asked.

"I am not Moses!" Gladys answered in desperation.

"Of course you aren't, Ai-weh-deh," the young girl said, "but Jehovah is still God! You have told us that countless times. If he is God, he can open the river for us."[5]

Gladys saw that the same God who had personally "qualified" this former parlor maid and transformed her into one of the most beloved missionaries in China could do what was impossible for man or woman. Gladys still didn't see the way of escape. She did not know *how* the Lord would come through, but with that fresh revelation, she no longer doubted that he was able.

With her focus shifted from the impossible circumstances to the power of God, Gladys and Sualan knelt at the shore of the river and asked God to open the vast waters for them. Then she gathered the children to sing hymns to keep their minds off their hungry stomachs.

A short time later, a Chinese nationalist army officer scouting the river heard a sound he thought was the whirring of an airplane. As he listened more closely, he realized it was the sound of children singing. After he found them and talked with the small woman leading them, he saw their predicament. Then he called a boat from the other side of the river. After several trips back and forth across the river, Gladys and every orphan got safely to the other side!

Still the journey was not nearly over. God had delivered them across the vast Yellow River, yet they faced many harrowing days and nights before they reached the safety of an orphanage. Gladys lay deathly ill for weeks following the journey, but she eventually recovered and went on to have many more years of fruitful ministry in China.

## Catching a Fresh Vision of Jesus

The hope-filled words of truth about the character of God that Sualan spoke infused Gladys with the supernatural courage she needed to persevere in the face of overwhelming obstacles. Your impossible situation probably will not be traversing a war-torn country with one hundred orphans in tow, but all of us face circumstances in our lives where things seem impossible. A teenager on drugs. A broken marriage. Financial troubles. We may be at the end of our resources, unable to do anything in our own efforts. Yet God is still God. As we fix our eyes on the one who can move the mountains or take us through them, part the sea or bring a boat out of nowhere to take us across, he makes us able to "do all things through Christ who strengthens us" (see Phil. 4:13). Like Gladys, we first need a fresh revelation of our Savior. Here's what we can learn from the life of this remarkable woman:

*Be honest with God.* If circumstances have obscured the face of God and all you see are the walls of impossibility surrounding you, admit it. Pretending to be strong or keeping up outward appearances just blocks fresh experiences of God's amazing grace. I love Psalm 62:8 because it gives us permission to "pour out your heart to him, for God is our refuge." This is an invitation to be real and honest with God about how desperate you are, holding nothing back.

As Bill Hybels says in *The God You're Looking For,* "In a curious way, the passwords that open the gates into the refuge of God are the soul-wrenching words that flow out of our hearts . . . when we tell Him how bad it really is and how close to the edge we really are. Somewhere in the middle of taking that step of faith, the gates open, and God's wings extend."[6] We are drawn close to God not when we pretend everything's okay or keep going in fast-forward in our own efforts but when we lay it all down before him. Tell God how you feel, and share it with another person so that she can pray for you. This kind of honesty truly can open the door to a fresh encounter with God.

*Be open to the input of others.* When we are in a difficult situation, grieving a loss, or devastated by overwhelming circumstances, our feelings can overrule the truth that we once learned about God. We even may forget how he has proved himself over and over again in the past. In Gladys Aylward's moment of desperation, God revealed himself through the words of a child. In a similar way God can use an unlikely person in our lives to show us something new about his character. I don't know who the catalyst might be for you; it might be a new believer, your teenager, a neighbor, or a Bible study leader. God can revive our hearts through a radio program or an encounter with a stranger if we are willing to listen. Receiving the input and counsel of others may open the door to a fresh vision of Jesus.

PART 3

A Fresh Vision
*of* Jesus through
Trials

# TEN

# Climbing into God's Lap

*Jesus invites you and me, in His name, to come into His Father's presence through prayer, crawl up into His lap by faith, put our heads on His shoulder of strength, feel His loving arms of protection around us, call Him "Abba" Daddy, and pour out our hearts to Him.*

ANNE GRAHAM LOTZ[1]

The last rays of the sun were going down as I sat in the living room of a friend's house with seven other women. We had prayed for the youth of our city, for our own teens and college kids, for the rocky marriage of one of the women, and for other issues. Everybody else was feeling lighthearted now, but I was still burdened about finances, work deadlines, and a struggle our daughter was experiencing.

Sitting next to me, Susan sensed my heaviness and said, "Just climb into God's lap. Let him put his arms around you and hold you."

*What an odd thing,* I thought. *Climb into God's lap?* No matter how hard I tried, I could not relate to that picture of God or visualize myself doing that. It sounded wonderful, but I had no concept of the kind of God you could snuggle up to. I could relate to an Almighty I could endeavor to please or serve. But climbing up into his lap and resting in his arms?

The group broke up and we hurried to our minivans, but those strange words kept going through my mind: "Climb into God's lap." As the months wore on, my dilemma continued. I could relate to a God I could be obedient to and please—but could I cuddle up on his lap?

When I'd read my Bible daily and was "prayed up" and happy-hearted enough to encourage others around me, I found it easier to approach him. But when I felt negative or sad, it was harder to receive his comforting love. And if something bad or terribly stressful had happened, I had a tendency to feel that God had abandoned me.

I gradually realized that how I saw God was connected to how I related to my father and stepfather. Papa showed his love by providing for and protecting us. He had a brilliant mind, and I admired and loved him—he was our hero! Papa was tall, dark, and handsome, a lawyer by trade and one of the top ten bridge players in the nation. He was the strong, silent type who didn't express affirmation or praise very readily.

I tried so hard to please Papa and be noticed by him, acting as "good" as I possibly could. But it was hard to gain his attention as the middle of six children—flanked by three outstanding, beautiful older sisters (called "the big girls"); my darling, everybody's-favorite little sister; and Papa's much-awaited only son and namesake, George F. Heath Jr.

Papa had very high standards for his children ("You should make all As; you're all smart because you're Heaths") but wasn't the kind of daddy who invited you to run up, jump on his lap, and feel his arms around you. He expected obedience, and since I'd seen his anger when he was crossed, I wanted to avoid his temper at all costs.

When he died in the middle of the night of a massive heart attack when I was eleven years old, I was left with the profound sense of abandonment a daughter experiences when she loses her father at an early age, whether by death or divorce.

With my mother's remarriage less than two years later, the filter through which I saw God got even more blurry. My stepfather was more my mother's husband than a father to us and was difficult to trust. One of his first memorable acts was taking the little terrier my dad had given my little sister Marilyn and me to a deserted country road and dumping him while we were at school. We never saw our beloved "Mr. Pup" again.

As I began to realize how my father filters had marred my picture of God, I began taking a hard look at father issues in my life. I began the process of releasing my faulty views of God and asking him to reveal himself to me anew. I also found support in a small group and some sessions with an insightful counselor. Over time I began to lay down my misrepresentations of God, forgive my father and stepfather, and focus on what God said about himself through his Word.

As I sought God in these simple ways by faith, not because I had a lot of feelings, what I knew about God in my head moved to my heart. I began to sense the loving arms of my heavenly Father—arms that had been there all along, waiting to welcome me in the best of times and the worst of times. I felt his acceptance just as I was, whether that was tired or in turmoil. I didn't have to work for him or try harder to please him. I didn't have to achieve or wipe my tears and put on a happy face. I could simply *be* and experience him as my comfort and refuge. I found the amazing good news that God wasn't going to abandon me in the middle of the night or when things got difficult but promised never to leave me or forsake me (Heb. 13:5).

As I saw anew the one who had created me and loved me, I found a new release in prayer and a deeper sense of his presence. I realized that he didn't love me less when I was broken or sad. In fact, the Bible says he is close to the brokenhearted and saves those who are crushed in spirit (Ps. 34:18). He is the Father who comforts us in all our troubles (2 Cor. 1:3–4). I discovered his open arms are ready to console and embrace when we are battered by life or circumstances, for he has said, "I will comfort you there as a child is comforted by its mother" (Isa. 66:13).

Because we live in a fallen world, no matter how good our earthly fathers and mothers are, they are imperfect and sometimes even misrepresent God. God wasn't like my father or stepfather, and he isn't exactly like your dad either. He is the perfect Father (Matt. 5:48). His love isn't available to us only when we measure up to rigid, hard-to-reach demands. And we don't have to perform to earn his love.

## Catching a Fresh Vision of Jesus

How do you see God? As a stern, unbending judge or policeman? As someone who, like your father, is looking to criticize your faults or who might abandon you unless you straighten up and fly right? Does the word *father* bring up negative or positive feelings in you? We will never escape a sense of futility and frustration until we begin to see what our Father God is really like and what his purposes are.[2] Here are some ways to begin:

*Understand how the father flaws in your life obscure your view of God.* God is the complete expression of love (1 John 4:16) who is infinitely patient and eternally faithful. We already have the Lord's attention; we don't have to jump through hoops to gain it! He chose you when he planned creation (Eph. 1:11), and his Word says, "See how great a love the Father has bestowed on us that we should be called children of God, and such we are" (1 John 3:1).

Martin Luther, father of the Reformation, understood this concept of a God who comforts us as a child on the lap of her mother and described prayer as the "climbing up of the heart into the heart of God." But many of us don't experience God as truly "the God of all comfort" (2 Cor. 1:3 NIV) because of the father flaws in our lives.

What can we do about the marred filters through which we see God? The first thing is to understand them and then to resolve them. Jack Frost, author of *Experiencing the Father's Embrace,* says that until the father issues are resolved through "an experiential revelation of the heavenly Father's love," a person may be a Christian for many years but find it difficult to experience the affectionate love God has for us.

For example, he describes *passive fathers* who may be at home but not really "home" in terms of being emotionally available and openhearted. Uncomfortable expressing emotion, they are short on hugs, kisses, and loving words. While not actually rejecting their kids, these fathers don't embrace their kids either. If you had a passive dad, your relationship with God may be characterized by obligation and duty rather than joy and a sense of being loved.

Fathers who are performance-oriented love their children, but that love is usually tied to measuring up to hard-to-reach expectations and demands for perfect obedience and success. Frequent criticism that isn't tempered with love and praise leaves kids feeling depressed, feeling like a failure, and relating to God in a performance-oriented way.

Absentee dads are not physically in the home because of death, divorce, or abandonment (this includes 50 percent of kids in America, and up to 70 percent for African American children). Children with an absentee dad may have the double whammy of a stepfather who doesn't meet their emotional needs or is undependable. In their relationship with God, even as adult Christians, they fear that God may not be there for them.

Authoritarian fathers put a higher priority on law than love. They require their children to follow every rule and may use fear, guilt, or intimidation to control them. If you were raised by an authoritarian dad, you may see God as a sheriff or master who is more to be feared and obeyed than enjoyed.

Any kind of abuse from fathers—verbal, emotional, physical, or sexual—creates a deep wound in the heart of the child. Besides struggling with guilt, shame, and low self-worth, abusive fathers leave their daughters feeling fearful and distrustful of God, ministers, and men in general (even into adulthood). Under all those damaging emotions is a seething anger at God.[3]

Our father can also shape our view of God in a positive way. Max Lucado said that by his dad's provision for him and his family, his stability and even temperament, he shaped his perspective of God. "When I imagine a faithful, unchanging God, who isn't moody or temperamental, I can do it because I saw this in my father." Though they weren't rich, his father was a good provider so he had an image that "God's job is also to see we have our basic needs of life provided for."[4]

You may be thinking that dads just can't win. In a way that's right; we live in an imperfect world, and no father can ever meet our every need and be the perfect father. Only God can fill that role! But the good news is that the very holes in our life that result from imperfect fathering or life's losses can be used to draw us into the arms of God. We can realize that our parents were probably doing the best that they could for the people they were at the time. And we can find freedom as we forgive them in every area they failed us.

*Draw a "God and me picture."* Take a piece of paper and draw a picture that reflects how you feel about God and relate to him and how he feels about you. Be honest as you visually portray your relationship with God. Then share your picture with a friend or spiritual mentor. Ask that person to draw her own "God and me" picture and share with you. When one woman drew such a picture, she depicted a knight sitting on a white horse and dressed in royal robes, as she walked behind him in tattered servants' clothing. Another drew herself seated next to Jesus at her kitchen table in intimate conversation over coffee. When our oldest son, then sixteen, was asked to draw this during a family devotional time, he left it blank. Seeing the reality of his distance from God got me on my knees even more for him. You can learn a tremendous amount about how to pray for a friend or family member when you understand where he or she is coming from.

*Bring your faulty view of God to the cross.*[5] What kind of filter has colored your vision of God? Review the categories of fathers in the paragraphs above. Then compare that view to how the Bible depicts God. Good places to start are Psalms 23, 103, 139, 145, and 146. If your perspective of God doesn't line up with the truth of Scripture, let me encourage you to bring it to the cross. Ask the Holy Spirit to clean off your filter in a prayer like, *"Lord, I want to know you as you really are. I want to come home to an intimate, trusting, loving relationship with you. Cleanse my filter. Heal the wounds in my heart from the 'father flaws' I've experienced. In every situation I go through, may my vision of you and your flawless character grow and grow, and may I be changed in the process."*

Regardless of how adequate or inadequate your earthly father was, you don't have to remain stuck in the perception of God you've carried around since childhood. You can be set free by the power of the cross. God is inviting you to come into his presence through prayer, crawl into his lap by faith, put your head on his shoulder, call him "Abba, Daddy," and pour out your heart to him. You can develop a close, loving relationship with your heavenly Father through his Son Jesus, who gave his life for you and who is the exact representation of the Father (Heb. 1:3). And you can enjoy him forever!

# ELEVEN

# The Lord Who Sees Me

*God sees you as much as if there were nobody else in
the world for Him to look at.*
                                        CHARLES SPURGEON

Thirteen-year-old Terri waved good-bye to her parents as she stood on the porch of her grandma's house in Canada, far away from where she had been raised in Brazil. Tears fell down her cheeks and a knot formed in her stomach, one so tight that it didn't go away for many years.

Terri was an "MK," or missionary kid, who grew up with her six siblings in a lush green lumber and cattle state of southern Brazil, where her parents served for most of their lives. As a young teen, she and her sister and brother were left in Canada with an elderly grandmother while her parents went back to Brazil—back to the work and ministry that was always their first priority.

Throughout her childhood, Terri lacked the security of feeling unconditionally loved and accepted. She felt little warmth or affection, as her parents held their children to high standards of performance. Her parents' discipline for minor infractions felt harsh and severe, and sadly they offered few signs of forgiveness or assurance. So Terri and her siblings grew to know God as severe, demanding, and distant—to be feared but not embraced, to be obeyed but never enjoyed. They were all expected to grow up to be missionaries, and Terri aimed to please. She attended church faithfully and even worked for a mission organization after her marriage. She was content being a "good" Christian.

Until tragedy struck.

"I don't know what I'd do if anything ever happened to my husband," Terri had casually commented to a friend one August afternoon. "He helps me so much. I'm spoiled."

She scurried home that day just in time to kiss Bob good-bye before he left for his night job. Bob was working the night shift as an electronics technician for a computer manufacturing company and planned to begin further schooling in September. To save money, he rode a motorcycle to work.

At four o'clock in the morning, something woke Terri up. She reached for her husband. He wasn't there. Suddenly she was wide awake, her heart racing. He had been due home at three.

The next several hours blurred into a maze of questions coupled with the stubborn self-assurance that God wouldn't let anything happen to Bob. As night became dawn and broke into full daylight, fear slowly knotted Terri's whole being.

Six o'clock. Seven o'clock. *Where is he?*

"O Lord, I'm desperate," she cried. "Please let me know where Bobby is."

Turning on the radio for comfort, she listened to a traffic report. Then she heard it. "An injured motorcyclist is being treated at USC Medical Center."

Questions without answers tumbled over each other in her spinning head. Shaking, she dialed the hospital.

"Yes, there's a Bob Geary here," the receptionist drawled. "But I can't tell you anything. You're gonna have to call later."

Struggling to hold her tears back, Terri dressed, fed her children, and arranged for their care so she could go to the hospital.

"Mrs. Geary," the doctor said brusquely in the emergency room waiting area. "Your husband's spinal cord is severely injured. He is paralyzed from the shoulders down. And if he lives, he'll never walk again."

*If he lives? Paralyzed? Never walk?* Disbelief, confusion, shock, and anger flooded over her. *He's wrong! God wouldn't let this happen!*

Terri was directed to the ICU waiting room to wait until she was allowed to see Bob. Friends stood by silently, and she was encouraged by their fervent prayers.

In the hours that followed, the story was pieced together from newspaper and TV reports and Bob's limited input: He left work at 2:00 A.M. Halfway home on the freeway, he looked up just in time to see an eighteen-wheeler falling off an overpass. To avoid being crushed to death, he bailed out from his bike. As his motorcycle disappeared under the truck, Bob hit the pavement, breaking his neck.

It was several days before Terri realized that if her husband recovered, he would be a quadriplegic. She hadn't the slightest idea what that meant for their life and family. In her numbness she couldn't know how deep the anger, depression, self-pity, and sorrow would become.

Life had been splintered forever.

As they left the hospital many months later, Terri and Bob joined the lonely world of the disabled, a world loaded with frustrations, discrimination, and stigma foreign to them. The daily invasion of nurses who cared for Bob, the constant waiting on him and their three children, assuming two parents' roles, and extreme fatigue all became sources of despair for Terri. And she was deeply afraid of the future.

Struggling with the challenges of life with a quadriplegic husband, Terri dreaded each morning. She yearned for trouble-free days and longed to fly away and be at rest.

One day she read the story of Hagar in Genesis 16. Pregnant with Abraham's firstborn son, she was mistreated by Sarai, so she ran away. Hagar ran as far as she could, but an angel sent by God caught up with her near a spring in the desert, beside the road to Shur. When the angel inquired where Hagar had come from and where she was going, Hagar answered, "I'm running away from my mistress" (v. 8).

*That's what I want to do—run away, far from the constant caretaking, the financial struggles, the ever-present weariness and burdens I face 24-7.* She felt betrayed by a distant, hard-to-reach God. Her head knew all the right things about God, but her heart felt he was a million miles away. One day she felt like she'd make it; the next day she was down in the depths, angry at herself, Bob, and most of all God.

All it took to trigger resentment was for the attendant to fail to show up or some other key need to not be met. *Why us? Why so many extra problems? Why this stupid wheelchair anyway?* Sometimes she hated that wheelchair and all it represented. And like Hagar, she just wanted to find a place to hide and rest.

As Terri pondered the story, she was struck by what the angel told Hagar—to go back to her mistress and submit to her (v. 9). The angel left her with a promise that God would increase her descendants until they would be too numerous to count. "You are the God who sees me," Hagar responded. "I have now seen the One who sees me" (v. 13 NIV).

In that moment Terri realized that God saw her just as he did Hagar in the desert. She wasn't a second-class citizen or one who was forgotten by God. He remembered her, and he would revive her and be with her as he was with Hagar.

As Terri began seeing Jesus as someone to run *to* instead of *away from*—as her refuge in her daily battles instead of an adversary trying to punish her—her heart began to be transformed. Instead of staying bitter, she began a journey of getting to know God in the midst of the challenges. She realized she had a choice: She could treat God as a harsh, severe villain and angrily grit her teeth while stumbling through her day alone. Or she could lean on God, who longed to be her comforter, her helper, and her peace-giver. It wasn't an overnight fix. The process of learning to lean on the "God of all grace" (1 Peter 5:10 NIV) was excruciatingly slow. With each cry of surrender, her aching heart would declare, "Okay, Lord Jesus, I accept your will for me today. I'm weak . . . but I'm grasping hold of your strength."

When she offered herself to him in this way, he drew near with his strength. Through encouraging calls, time spent with gentle friends who listened without judging, notes in the mail, timely radio programs, and simply spending time alone with God, he revealed his presence and love.

Although she sometimes needs to re-surrender herself to God, Terri has found that the secret to experiencing his strength comes in trusting him daily in the struggles that emerge. It's one day at a time.

Now no longer was God distant and hard to reach. He hadn't abandoned her. And he did see right where she was. Terri finally began to experience the reality of Psalm 73:28, "but as for me, it is good to be near God. I have made the Sovereign LORD my Refuge" (NIV).

God graciously brought Bob far beyond medical expectations. Eventually he learned to feed himself and drive his own electric chair as well as a custom-built van. He donated countless hours of technical advice to missions and became a self-made "computer guru," offering his expertise to many who couldn't afford to take their computers out to be fixed. After battling acute leukemia, Bob died this past year.

"Looking back, even with the trials, I wouldn't want to return to just sailing along and being a good Christian but not really knowing God," says Terri twenty-four years after Bob's accident. Over and over again the struggles she and her husband experienced became a doorway to a fresh vision of Jesus, to seeing that he is her strength when she's weak, her provider when the family has need, her rest when she's weary. She knows her Lord in an intimate way *because of* the trials and difficulties. And she knows that the God who sees her loves her with an everlasting love.[1]

Maybe you feel, like Terri did, that God has ignored you or is too busy to care about the pain in your life. The truth is, "God sees you as much as if there were nobody else in the world for Him to look at," said Charles Spurgeon. "If I have as many people as there are here to look at, of course my attention must be divided. But the infinite mind of God is able to grasp a million objects at once and yet to focus as much on one as if there were nothing else but that one. . . . God sees you with all His eyes, with the whole of His sight—you—*you*—You—YOU! are the particular object of His attention at this very moment."[2]

Whether we feel like it or not, we are an open book to God, and he knows our every thought. He counts the number of hairs on our head. And there is no place we can go to avoid his Spirit or be out of his sight. If we climb to the sky, he's there. If we go underground, he's there. If we could fly on morning's wings to the farthest horizon, we would find that he is already there waiting! We are never out of his sight (see Ps. 139 MESSAGE).

## Catching a Fresh Vision of Jesus

If God can see you, he can hear you. He hears your prayers, and even if you can't get a word out, he understands your tears and sighs. In the middle of the night when no one is around to care for you, God is there with you. He's not slumbering or sleeping, even if the rest of the world is (see Ps. 121:4). What good news—we are not alone. We are known and loved by the Lord! Here are some ways to get a fresh glimpse of this aspect of God:

*Reflect on when you feel invisible, discounted, and forgotten.* What triggers in you a sense that God has left you or is too busy with his work in the universe to care about your problems? For Terri it was a tragedy that altered her life and her family. For others it might be a divorce, the loss of a loved one, a financial reversal, or a job layoff. Bring these past or present experiences to God and tell him you want to regain your spiritual eyesight and a sense of his presence. Then meditate on Psalm 139, Acts 17:28, and Matthew 10:29–30.

No matter how difficult the trial you may go through, learn to "cheerfully expect that He, before whom you stand, will ever guide you with His eye; will support you by His guardian hand; will keep you from all evil; and 'when you have suffered a while, will make you perfect, will establish, strengthen, and settle you' (1 Peter 5:10) and then 'preserve you unblamable unto the coming of our Lord Jesus Christ' (1 Thess. 5:23)!"³

*Seek the face of God in the midst of trouble.* When was the last time you looked for Jesus in the midst of a pressing problem? Often we say, "Lord, fix this. Change this problem. Do something about this mess I'm in!" That's okay, yet I've found we can grow by praying the life-transforming prayer, "Lord, I don't understand this situation, and I seem powerless to change it. But I want to see you and encounter you. Would you teach me what you want me to know about *you* through this? Would you draw me near and show me what special life lessons and revelations of your grace you want me to experience?"

I've found the most growth happened when my focus moved from whatever problem I faced to asking, seeking, and being open to something the Lord wanted to reveal to me about himself. Seeing a fresh vision of Jesus that focuses on his character, his sufficiency, and *who he is* instead of how I want things to change makes all the difference.

# TWELVE

# I've Just Seen Jesus!

*The man who has seen Jesus can never be daunted. . . .*
*Nothing can turn the man who has seen Him; he en-*
*dures "as seeing Him Who is invisible."*

OSWALD CHAMBERS

Martha pulled the rough brown shawl around her head as she arranged fruit on a wooden tray, hauled water from the well to fill the pitchers, and did the countless tasks necessary to prepare a meal for her dearest friend, Jesus. She paused a moment to look out the window to the road for her expected visitors. Jesus and his disciples, on their way to Jerusalem, would be stopping by the village soon.

As always Martha, her sister Mary, and her brother Lazarus would warmly welcome them into their home. She wanted everything to be perfect and ready for their arrival.

Jesus had different relationships with different people during his time on earth, depending on their hunger for him and God's purposes. The multitudes heard his teachings and were desperate for the "bread" he offered; countless people were healed by his touch and delivered from oppressing spirits. But the multitudes didn't have an intimate relationship with the Messiah.

The disciples traveled, ate, and spent time with Jesus. They didn't just hear his teachings and parables; he told them the principles behind the stories.

But there was something special about Jesus' relationship with Martha, Mary, and Lazarus. Along with John, they were some of Jesus's favorite people, those he was closest to and loved best. That's what made it all the more frustrating and deeply distressing to Martha that Jesus didn't come when the sisters sent an urgent message telling him, "Master, the one you love so very much is sick."

She just *knew* he would come since he and the disciples were only two miles away, in Jerusalem. Because Jesus had a powerful ability to heal and great affection for Lazarus, she had no doubt that before long they'd see Jesus walking up the dusty road to Bethany and Lazarus would be well again.

For days Martha had labored over her brother's sickbed, wringing her hands in worry and watching at the window. *Surely Jesus got the message. Nothing could prevent him from coming,* she thought. But their beloved teacher didn't show up. And nothing they did seemed to help Lazarus. No amount of hot soup or medicinal herbs revived him.

Finally the two sisters watched as the color drained from their brother's face, the life dissipating before their eyes as his body grew cold and stiff. Martha and Mary collapsed in a flood of tears. Added to their grief were the painful questions: "Why didn't our friend Jesus come? This would have all been different if he'd been here! It would only have taken a word, a touch, and Lazarus would have recovered. Didn't Jesus care enough to walk the two miles from Jerusalem to help us?"

They didn't have the big picture. They didn't know that when Jesus got the message, he said, "This sickness is not fatal. It will become an occasion to show God's glory by glorifying God's Son."

After waiting two days, Jesus told his disciples to go back to Judea. They tried to convince him not to go because the Jews were out to kill him, but he wasn't deterred.

"Our friend Lazarus has fallen asleep. I'm going to wake him up," Jesus announced.

When he finally headed for Bethany, Lazarus had been dead four days. By this time many Jews were already there, comforting Mary and Martha and mourning with them. Since Martha heard through the grapevine that Jesus was coming, she raced out to meet him while her sister stayed at home weeping.

"You don't have to wait for the End. I am, right now, Resurrection and Life. The one who believes in me, even though he or she dies, will live. And everyone who lives believing in me does not ultimately die at all. Do you believe this?" Jesus asked Martha.

"Yes, Lord!" said Martha. "I know and have always believed you are the Messiah, the Son of God. You are the one who has come into the world from God!" Not a bad response from one who hadn't yet seen his glory.

Moments later Mary was alerted that Jesus had arrived and ran out to him. She fell at his feet and echoed what Martha had said, "Master, if only you had been here, my brother would not have died."

"When Jesus saw her sobbing and the Jews with her sobbing, a deep anger welled up within him. He said, 'Where did you put him?'" Then Jesus wept. He wasn't weeping because Lazarus was dead or because he was sad for his friends Mary and Martha. He wept because the answer was standing among them, but they didn't see him.

"Well, if he loved him so much, why didn't he do something to keep him from dying? After all, he opened the eyes of a blind man," said the naysayers in the crowd.

Nobody could have scripted what happened next. Jesus gave the order to remove the stone, but Martha, ever the realist, objected, "Master, by this time there's a stench. He's been dead four days!"

Looking her in the eye, Jesus asked, "Didn't I tell you that if you believed, you would see the glory of God?

"Lazarus, come out!" Jesus shouted. And Lazarus emerged from the tomb; he looked like a cadaver, wrapped from head to toe, with a cloth over his face. Jesus said, "Unwrap him and let him loose."

Tears of joy flowed from Martha's and Mary's eyes when they saw their brother alive. Awe filled their hearts as they saw Jesus' majesty and glory displayed before them.[1]

## Catching a Fresh Vision of Jesus

Jesus is the way, the truth, and the life, and when we encounter him and see him as he is, we can't help but be changed just as Martha was. Let me encourage you:

*Be honest with God and ask him for what you need.* As usual, Martha didn't mince words. Some might say she was bold or arrogant to approach the Savior, but I have to say a few words in this woman's behalf. Often she gets a bad rap: Martha's the driven one, they say. She was the sister Jesus scolded when he said, "Martha, Martha, you are worried and distracted about many things," and pointed to sister Mary's devotion as the most important thing (and it is, by the way!). Mary was the more spiritual sister, and her priorities were right. Not like her busy, practical sister Martha!

But let's take another look at Martha. First, *she asked.* She didn't hesitate to send an SOS message to Jesus telling him she needed his help.

Second, she was honest. When he didn't come in time, she candidly declared, "Master, if you'd been here, my brother wouldn't have died. Even now, I know that whatever you ask God he will give you" (John 11:21–22 MESSAGE). Martha didn't yet know that the man standing before her had the power to raise her brother from the dead. Like most of those who walked and talked with Christ, she didn't fully understand who he was. Yet she had an irrepressible faith and confidence in her Lord. She didn't run from him when devastated over the loss of her brother—she ran *toward him.* In fact, she caught up with him on the road before he even entered the village.

*Don't sink into guilt* if you are more like Martha than Mary. Perhaps you've felt like a second-class Christian if you aren't like quiet, contemplative Mary who stopped everything to sit at the feet of Jesus. Maybe you feel guilty if you're often busy and distracted doing many things. If God wired you to run a children's ministry or a company and you always have so much on your plate that you can never get it all done, he understands. If you are a single parent and juggle multiple tasks and responsibilities, God knows how stretched your time is. Martha's serving was honorable, and when we do our work and service as unto the Lord, with our focus on him, he receives it as worship (see Col. 3:23–24).

You don't have to be someone you're not or try to change yourself to be more contemplative or spiritual. *Seeing and encountering Jesus* is how transformation happens. The Lord met Martha as she was, in the midst of her busy life and in the midst of her grief over losing her brother, and revealed himself to her. Just as he knew the longings of her heart, he knows the longings of your heart and will meet you as you lay them out before him.

*As Mary did, offer all you are to him.* He laid down his life that we might experience newness of life on this earth and life forever with him. When you turn over all of your being in joyful abandon, your life, though outwardly busy, will become a "living prayer"[2] and you will be increasingly aware of the Lord's presence. Give yourself completely—again or for the first time—to him who created you and loves you with an everlasting love. "I despair when I try to change myself and patch myself up," said Corrie ten Boom. "I can't do it and never will be able to do it, but if I surrender myself to Him who made me, I experience miracles!"[3]

How do we know Martha was transformed by this experience? The next and last time Martha is mentioned in the

Bible recounts the supper in her home in honor of Jesus and in celebration of Lazarus' resurrection. With guests crowded around their table, her sister Mary anointed the feet of Jesus with expensive perfume. Martha was still serving and was no less productive or hospitable, but her spirit had changed.

We read nothing about Martha being distracted over tasks or mentally anxious or bustling around. Her practical side didn't respond to Mary's lavish demonstration of devotion by saying, "No, Mary! We need the money for groceries!"—even though she probably contributed to purchasing the costly nard. She didn't side with Judas, who said the poor needed the offering more. Her heart was in agreement with this lavish display of worship.[4] Her focus was Jesus, and the vision of his glory had forever changed her.

# THIRTEEN

# The Joy
# *of* Obedience

*Take my will, and make it thine;*
*It shall be no longer mine.*
*Take my heart, it is Thine own;*
*It shall be Thy royal throne.*

FRANCES RIDLEY HAVERGAL

D on't make me go, Father! Not another religious con-
vention! I can't endure a whole week of being in
the tent all day and evening, hearing sermons and
hymns," nineteen-year-old Hannah Hurnard cried to her father.
For many years he had spent countless hours on his knees for
his daughter's salvation. Daily he had read her the Scriptures.
But nothing brought a change in Hannah. She was as lost and
miserable as ever.

Her father wanted her to go to Keswick meetings, certain that God would do something in her heart. To overcome her resistance, he made a bargain with her: she could spend most of the day hiking in the fields and riding her bicycle alone if she would go with him to only two Keswick meetings a day.

She thought it sounded like a good proposition, but as the week dragged on, Hannah's turmoil grew. In the middle of a meeting, she suddenly hurried out of the evangelistic tent and sped away on her bicycle to the boarding house they were staying in outside the town. An awful week of supercharged spiritual meetings and being surrounded by hundreds of radiant Christians made her feel further away from God and more wretched and alone.

Hannah had grown up in a strict Puritan home with parents who were completely devoted to Christ. Yet from her earliest years, she found church services dreary and depressing, the Bible a dead book that meant nothing, and herself the most miserable of creatures. A profound stuttering problem kept her from ordinary activities like riding on buses or shopping by herself because she couldn't engage in ordinary conversation. She was tormented by fears and ridiculed every day at school because of her stammer.

While other children in the neighborhood played games and sang, Hannah watched them from the window of her room. When her siblings went across town or out with friends, she stayed behind. Only if her parents were with her did she go out in the city. As a result, throughout her childhood and teenage years, she had no friends and no hope.

Worst of all, although she lived in a home where worshiping God was the most important aspect of life, God seemed unreal and unreachable. No amount of repenting or going to gospel services changed that. With every passing year Hannah sank deeper into despair, and one day she awoke so depressed that she longed to commit suicide if only she had the courage.

As Hannah biked away from the Keswick meeting to her room that day in 1924, she wanted more than anything to believe, just as all the missionaries she'd heard, her parents, and the throngs of Christians she'd met, that there was a God who could help her.

Falling on her knees beside her bed in desperation, she cried out, "O God, if there is a God anywhere, you must make yourself real to me. If you exist and are really what these people describe you to be, you can't leave me like this."[1]

A few moments later she opened the Bible to 1 Kings 18 and began to read about the standoff on Mount Carmel between Elijah and the prophets of Baal. Hannah was struck by what Elijah said to the people: "Come near to me" (v. 30 AMP). She was even more amazed by what he did. After the prophet repaired the broken altar of God, he laid the sacrifice on it.

She couldn't deny the truth any longer. She must bring herself to the altar, yielding her entire being and her stammering tongue to God.[2] But this was more than she could bear. What if it led to her worst nightmare, standing before an audience paralyzed by fear, unable to get a word out? How could she surrender to a God who would put her through this kind of pain? It was impossible.

Her eyes went to the next verses: "Then the fire of the Lord fell, and consumed the burnt sacrifice, and the wood, and the stones, and the dust, and licked up the water that was in the trench. And when all the people saw it, they fell on their faces: and said, 'The Lord, he is God! the Lord, he is God!'" (v. 39 AMP).

Suddenly a burst of light flooded into the dark, tormented heart of this young British woman, and Jesus revealed himself to her in such a tangible way that the sense of his presence never left her the rest of her life. She expressed this intimate encounter with Christ in poetic verse:

> I have seen the face of Jesus,
> Tell me naught of earth beside,
> I have heard the voice of Jesus,
> And my soul is satisfied.[3]

Hannah was just as sure that Christ stood beside her as if she'd seen him with her eyes. He loved her and had come to tell her that he wanted her and would use her, even with her stuttering problem.

When she got up from her knees, she was a different girl, one who "for the first time in her life felt joy, felt secure, felt able to laugh, could have clapped her hands and danced for sheer ecstasy of heart."[4]

She had been in church countless times and heard others talk about God. But now she had seen the Lord for herself. In this thirty-minute encounter with Christ, Hannah Hurnard was transformed. "It was as though a miserable, stunted plant had suddenly been transplanted from a flowerpot, into a sunny, richly fertilized flowerbed. I was lifted out of the dreadful isolation of self-imprisonment and set down into the love of God."[5]

She still needed to experience much character and spiritual growth, but with this fresh vision of Jesus, Hannah began to be changed from the inside out. Her purpose became to serve the Lord she loved wherever he guided her and to develop "a hearing heart," attentive and obedient to his every word. Her obedience led to a life of joyous, daily communion with God, a vibrant literary career, and a ministry in the United Kingdom and the Middle East that spanned several decades.

## Catching a Fresh Vision of Jesus

Perhaps God has seemed unreal to you, as he did to nineteen-year-old Hannah. You've prayed, but you don't hear the answers you're looking for. You've looked in all the right places—and maybe even some wrong places—but he seems far away. Yet you long to know and encounter his love. We can learn so much from the experience of Hannah Hurnard that can open our eyes to a fresh glimpse of the Lord Jesus:

*Offer yourself as a living sacrifice.* Christ himself was the sacrifice, giving his life for us when we were still sinners (Rom. 5:8), yet he calls us to give ourselves to him. In other words, *put yourself on the altar* as Hannah did that day at Keswick, just as she was—stammer, fears, and all. "Take your every-day, ordinary life—your sleeping, eating, going-to-work, and walking-around life—and place it before God as an offering. Embracing what God does for you is the best thing you can do for him. . . . Fix your attention on God. You'll be changed from the inside out. Readily recognize what he wants from you, and quickly respond to it" (Rom. 12:1–2 MESSAGE).

*Allow God to exchange your weakness for his strength.* After Hannah's encounter with Christ, her thinking, perspective, and heart were completely new. She still had many of the same basic struggles. Fear of heights, the dark, crowds, becoming ill and losing consciousness, death, and even people plagued her. And her stammer still disabled her communication with others.

Yet the foundational verse of her life became, "My grace is sufficient for thee: for my strength is made perfect in weakness" (2 Cor. 12:9 KJV). Hannah Hurnard found that as she yielded her stuttering mouth to Christ, he gave her his strength and ability to speak. The first time she addressed a Bible school audience, she was overwhelmed by physical panic. But instead of being paralyzed by her fears as she had been so many times in her life, she ignored the fears and began to speak. Suddenly she felt like Jesus was next to her, speaking through and for her. She communicated her message without a stammer.

Those who heard her that day and over the years as she served as an evangelist in the United Kingdom and the Holy Land felt that God had given her a gift of speaking. In regular conversation, her stammer remained. But when she witnessed in factories, missions, Wimbledon Common, church meetings, or hospitals, the stammer was never apparent.

Hannah was pressed into an "utter dependence" on the Lord because of her affliction. You and I may not have a problem with stuttering, but each of us must come to our own utter dependence on Christ, no matter what our weaknesses or strengths are. Hannah learned to walk by faith and always go forward as though she could see the Lord next to her reminding her, "My grace is sufficient for thee: for my strength is made perfect in weakness" (2 Cor. 12:9 KJV).

What weaknesses hinder you from pursuing God's purpose for your life? Is it fear? A sense of inadequacy? Is it an inability to speak, like it was for Hannah Hurnard? A dread of disapproval or failure? A sin that you haven't overcome? List your hindrances and then give them to God, one by one, asking him to make his strength perfect in your weakness.

*Walk in obedience, knowing that an obedient heart is a hearing heart.* From the first moments that Jesus made himself real to her, Hannah decided to speak to him, ask him questions, and act in every way as she would if she could actually see him. Even when she felt no assurance or began to doubt, she still focused on Christ and acted and obeyed as though she saw him visibly present.[6]

"As we begin to focus upon God, the things of the spirit will take shape before our inner eyes," said A. W. Tozer. "Obedience to the word of Christ will bring an inward revelation of the Godhead. It will give acute perception enabling us to see God even as is promised to the pure in heart. A new God-consciousness will seize upon us and we shall begin to taste and hear and inwardly feel God, who is our life and our all. More and more, as our faculties grow sharper and more sure, God will become to us the great All, and His presence the glory and wonder of our lives."[7]

Jesus spoke clearly of the relationship between obeying God and seeing him: "Those who obey my commandments are the ones who love me. And because they love me, my Father will love them, and I will love them. And I will reveal myself to each one of them" (John 14:21).

As Hannah obeyed out of love, Jesus did reveal himself time after time. "Although at first every obedience looked impossible and I felt sick with fright as I tried to stammer out to my friends and family of the new faith that had come to me, *the same overwhelming sense of the reality of his presence always followed every act of obedience*," Hannah explained (emphasis mine).

This principle applied not just to her speaking but to her entire ministry. After serving for years in Palestine, she and other missionaries were evacuated due to impending war and furloughed in England for an extended time. She longed to get back to her ministry to Jews and Arabs, but all the doors closed, and it looked impossible.

Then Hannah was offered a position as a housekeeper in a hospital in Palestine. At first she refused. "No, Lord! I couldn't do that! I'm terrible at housekeeping and this can't be the way to get back to Palestine. I'm an evangelist, not a housekeeper." But even though she confessed to the hospital administrator her lack of experience in housekeeping, God confirmed his call to her through letters of invitation and through his voice and Scripture, and she finally set out to obey.[8]

As Hannah flew back to the Holy Land three weeks later and took up the position of housekeeping director of the hospital, joy and gratitude overshadowed everything else. And through this unlikely position, God gave her countless opportunities to minister to both Jews and Arabs, even during wartime. The position even allowed her to remain in the country when scores of other Christians were cast out during another war. And always, as she obeyed, Jesus was as real to her as on that first day her heart was awakened.

What is God asking of you? What is his purpose for this season of your life? What steps has he directed you to take? Set your heart to obey him. Sign on the dotted line even before you know all the details. And you will find, just as Hannah Hurnard did, that the reality of his presence will grow in your experience and life as you develop a hearing heart and walk in obedience to what God asks of you.

# PART 4

# A Fresh Vision
# *of* Jesus through
# Mountaintop
# Experiences

# FOURTEEN

# The Great
# Physician

*We must realize that God's supreme purpose for granting
miracles is to reveal Himself. Healing is a witness to the
wonder of His Person. . . . Knowing God is the greatest
miracle resulting from our prayers of intercession.*

DICK EASTMAN
*LOVE ON ITS KNEES*

N*ot this weekend,* I thought as our boys raced in from
their Saturday play in the backyard. Hearing our six-
year-old wheezing loudly with each breath, I headed
for the kitchen to get his medicine.

When asthma afflicted our son, a big black cloud seemed
to settle over our house. Asthma had sent us to emergency
rooms, derailed one year's Christmas plans, and kept our son

from starting first grade with the rest of the kids. As our doctor explained it, controlling an asthma attack was like stopping a ball from rolling down a hill—you should catch it before it gets very far down the slope.

Even more than usual we wanted to head off this attack. My husband, Holmes, had scheduled a father-son trip to Dallas that included a day at Six Flags Over Texas, and they were leaving the next morning. Their bags were packed, and they were excited. But now this . . .

Our son's shortness of breath and violent round of coughing spurred me to work faster as I gathered up his inhaler, fluids, and medicines. *If all else fails, we'll call the doctor and head to his office or the emergency room.*

And somewhere in there, I knew, we'd say a prayer for him, but perhaps more as a last resort than as a first resource.

This time it was different. As Holmes and I talked about our son's condition and the special trip they'd planned, we were struck that maybe we'd been doing things backwards. The doctor, prescriptions, and medical help were all important. But why not call on God *first?*

I'd read that God is our Great Physician, but I'd never taken it seriously or heard any teaching about it. I'd never seen God heal someone, so I was somewhat of a skeptic. However, it seemed like a great alternative to what we'd been through countless times.

So, infused with just a mustard seed of hope and belief, we knelt beside our son on the couch and asked God to give us wisdom and show us how to pray. But doubts and questions began to distract my train of thought.

*Here I am asking God to heal our son, to touch his body and reverse this physical condition. But I don't really know what it says in the Bible about it. When does God heal, and how should we ap-*

*proach him? I know that when Jesus was on earth, he healed people with just a touch or word, but does he even do that today?*

We were novice Christians, enthusiastic about our growing faith. But we'd never heard any teaching from the pulpit or in a Sunday school class on healing. A compelling curiosity replaced the usual anxiety I felt when our son was sick. What *did* the Bible say about healing?

When I told Holmes what I was thinking, he said some of the same thoughts were running through his mind. Since by this time it was evening and bookstores were closed, we searched the house for books that might have a chapter on healing and prayer. I checked the shelves in the family room and a cabinet in the garage, where I found a study that was just what we were looking for: *What the Bible Says about Healing.* I had bought it months before but had gotten busy and tucked it away without reading it.

Now I opened it eagerly. Our son's coughing had subsided and he'd fallen asleep temporarily, so we put our Bibles at the kitchen table, filled our coffee cups, and dove into the recommended verses. We read Isaiah 53:4–5, "Surely he took up our infirmities and carried our sorrows. . . . he was pierced for our transgressions, he was crushed for our iniquities; the punishment that brought us peace was upon him, and by his wounds we are healed" (NIV). In Psalm 30:2 we read, "O LORD my God, I called to you for help and you healed me" (NIV). We also read Psalm 103:3, Matthew 4:23, and other verses from the Old and New Testaments.

With each verse, my heart felt a surge of hope. Everything we were reading suggested that God actually can heal people—spiritually, emotionally, and physically. In fact, I discovered in Exodus 15:26 that one of his names is *Jehovah Rapha,* "the

Lord our healer." We found specific Scriptures to pray in times of sickness and began to realize that the timetable for healing was God's, but he invited us to cast our burdens and sicknesses upon him and to seek him on health issues.

Throughout the evening we continued to work on the one-hundred-page Bible study while our two younger children ate their dinner and played beside us in the kitchen. Later, after we'd read the kids a story and tucked them into bed, we refilled our coffee cups and returned to the Bible to complete our research. I knew the Bible held something, some piece of the puzzle God wanted to teach us, that we really needed. But I had no idea what it was.

At about three o'clock in the morning, we read one of the last verses in the study, James 5:14. The verse said that when someone was sick, Christians were to call the church elders to pray over him and anoint him with oil in the Lord's name. I'd never noticed that verse before. Elders praying for the sick? Anointing with oil? The church we attended didn't engage in that. I had heard the minister teach in our couples' Sunday school class that God *used* to do powerful things and Jesus healed people in his earthly ministry, but that was then and it was over.

While the passage sounded unusual to my ears, it seemed to point to this kind of prayer as part of God's prescription. Our hearts soared when we read the next verse: "And the prayer of faith will save him who is sick, and the Lord will restore him" (James 5:15 AMP).

"Holmes, this is it," I said, my excitement building. "It's the missing piece that's never been done for him before. We need to have some elders, someone who really believes God is powerful, come pray for him and do what these verses say."

As we thought about it, I remembered two young pastors from another local church we'd visited recently.

"Steve and Jeff! I'll bet they pray for sick people. Why don't we call them right now?" I said, feeling a sense of urgency.

"I don't know; it's the middle of the night. We'd wake them up," Holmes said.

"But doctors are on call in the middle of the night, so maybe elders are too if someone is sick. And if he doesn't get better through the night, we're going to be at the emergency room with him. Let's see if I can find a phone number."

A few minutes later I got Steve on the phone and explained the situation. He groggily but patiently listened as I told him about our son's asthma attack and what we'd just discovered in the Bible. "Would you and Jeff come pray for our son? James says 'call for the elders to pray,' and you're the only ones we know who would do this. . . . It's the one thing that's never been done for him, and we just know it would make a difference."

"I'll tell you what," Steve proposed. "I'll start praying now, and you all try to get a little sleep. We'll be over there in a little while."

We were so excited we couldn't sleep. Instead we stayed up the rest of the night, talking and waiting for the two pastors to arrive. My anticipation matched that of a child on Christmas Eve.

At 5:30 A.M. we heard a quiet knock on the door, and there stood Jeff and Steve with a guitar, Bibles, and a small vial of oil. We thanked them for coming and led them into the family room, where our son was resting on the couch.

"We'd like to pray for you and ask God to make you well. Would that be okay?" Jeff asked.

139

"Sure."

"We're going to touch your forehead here with a little oil, just like the Bible says," Jeff explained. As the two men began to pray, nothing happened immediately. But a profound sense of peace permeated the space all around us, and we felt as if we were wrapped in a quilt of God's comfort.

As they continued praying, our son relaxed and became very still. Then suddenly he called, "Mom, get a pan. I think I'm going to throw up!" In a few minutes the thick mucus that had been plugging his bronchial tubes came up—the very thing that happened when he was given Adrenalin shots in the emergency room. Only this time it wasn't a painful round of injections causing an adrenaline rush—it was God's power.

His breathing slowed down and the wheezing gradually subsided. In a short time he sat up and a rosy color came back into his cheeks. Steve led us in singing along with his guitar as the sun came up. God's presence filled the room and inflated our hearts with joy. I looked over at our son. His blue eyes were shining brightly, and his cheeks were flushed as if he'd just come in from playing G.I. Joe in the park instead of struggling all night with an asthma attack. A grin spread over his face as he said, "Dad, when are we leaving?"

As the men went out the door, our son asked me, "Did you see that, Mom? Did you see the angel standing beside me when Jeff and Steve were praying? He was very bright and shiny, all white and glowing. You must have seen it!"

We hadn't seen anything but the morning sun streaming in the windows and our son, who'd been sick but now was well. But that was enough to show us God's power and love.

Later that morning our little guy and his dad waved to me as they drove out of the driveway in the red VW van, just as they'd planned. After they left, I dressed our two other children in their Sunday best, and we headed for church.

As my voice blended with all the other voices at church that morning, my heart offered an irrepressible outpouring of thanksgiving for our wonderful, glorious Savior and Great Physician as we sang, "Blessed assurance, Jesus is mine! / O what a foretaste of glory divine! / . . . This is my story, this is my song, / praising my Savior, all the day long!" My joy was so full I couldn't contain the praise as I realized that the same Spirit who raised Jesus from the dead could actually bring life and health to our mortal bodies. He hadn't stopped doing what he did on earth: bringing good news to the afflicted (Isa. 61:1). The miracle we'd witnessed was wonderful, but seeing God revealing himself in the midst of us was perhaps even greater.

## Catching a Fresh Vision of Jesus

That day I discovered that God's healing power isn't locked into the distant past of Bible times but can come through the prayers of compassionate, believing people in our time as well. I never looked at healing or at the Lord in the same way after this experience. I realized that God *welcomes us* to his throne of grace not just for the problems we have but also for our physical ailments. I also began to discover that Jesus can heal people from crippling memories, past hurts, and emotional trauma. And I learned that when we ask for healing, we aren't asking for something outside of who the Lord is, because part of the essence of his being is Divine Healer. Healing is part of the outflow of his love to his people.

Not only did my faith rise exponentially as a result of seeing Jesus as the Great Physician, but my husband and I began to see healing prayer as a normal part of Christian life. Jesus had a burden for the sick and hurting, and he told those who followed him to be healers as well (Matt. 10:7–8). God began to bring us opportunities to pray for people who were sick and allowed us to witness God's healing in their lives—not because of anything about us, but because of who God is and our simple desire to be his conduits to a hurting world.

I love how *The Message* renders James 5:14–15:

> Are you hurting? Pray. Do you feel great? Sing. Are you sick? Call the church leaders together to pray and anoint you with oil in the name of the Master. Believing-prayer will heal you, and Jesus will put you on your feet.

We all experience needing Jesus to put us back on our feet. We can be a part of his work as we:

*Are willing to be a vehicle of God's healing mercy to others.* "God joyfully employs an infinite variety of means to bring health and well-being to his people," said Richard Foster. "We are glad for God's friends, the doctors, who with skill and compassion help our bodies fight against disease and sickness. . . . We also celebrate the growing army of women and men and children who are learning how to bring the healing power of Christ to others for the glory of God and the good of all concerned."[1]

Who do you know who is struggling with a physical illness and you could faithfully pray for every day? Write their names on an index card and put it in your Bible to remind you to stand in the gap for them. When you visit people at the hospital, try gently asking, "Could I pray for you right now?" instead of saying, "I'll keep you in my prayers." I've seen very few people turn that invitation down.

*Study God's Word* and ask his Spirit to teach you how to pray effectively for those around you who are suffering. Look up, read, and meditate on these verses:

- Matthew 10:7–8
- Genesis 20:17
- Psalm 107:19–20
- John 9:1–27
- James 5:13–18
- 2 Chronicles 7:14
- Psalm 147:3
- Proverbs 3:7–8
- Luke 9:11
- Acts 9:32–35

Jot down beside each passage what you learn about healing from reading it. As you learn to bathe your prayers with Scripture, you'll experience miracles in your life and the lives of those you pray for. And since Jesus Christ is at the right hand of the Father interceding for us day and night, when you pray for others, you are joining him in his full-time profession, which naturally brings a fresh intimacy with him.

We don't know God's timetable or whether a person will gain wholeness and health on this earth or in heaven (where we will all receive new, perfect bodies), but we can bring ourselves and those we are concerned for to the throne of grace and do the things he told us in his Word to do and thus receive the Spirit's renewing power. As you do, you will catch a fresh vision of Christ as he heals the bodies, minds, and emotions of yourself and others.

# FIFTEEN

# A Light in the Darkness

*The only Christ for whom there is a shred of evidence is a miraculous figure making stupendous claims.*

C. S. Lewis

The digital clock on Emily's bedside table flashed 4:00 A.M. She pulled herself upright, her nightgown damp with perspiration. *Another nightmare.* The darkness outside the window seemed to have crept into her soul. She heard nothing from the normally busy street below. New York City, the city that never sleeps, didn't bother to wake up with her in these nighttime vigils. Flipping on the light, she slipped into her robe and headed to her studio. She sank down onto a stool with a sigh and ran her hands over the smooth wood and cold metal of the sculpture she'd worked on until midnight.

Too soon, she glanced at the clock and saw that it was time to get ready for her 6:00 A.M. workout at the gym. Donning exercise clothes and tying her tennis shoes, she headed downtown. She shook her head as she thought about Lauren, the woman she'd recently met in the locker room. Lauren called herself a Christian. *Christian.* What a strange word. In all her thirty-seven years Emily had never before met anyone who called herself a Christian. She shuddered as she thought of the stereotypes she'd seen on the news. Christians, she thought, were usually part of a dangerous political group. Lauren didn't *seem* dangerous. But she was different.

That morning after their workout, Emily said, "Lauren, you seem like a pretty cool person. You must be mistaken about being a Christian."

"But I *am* a Christian!" Lauren explained. "And it's not political. It means I love God, my Savior Jesus Christ."

Emily cringed, tempted to put her hand over Lauren's mouth. They were in a downtown New York City gym full of healthy, liberal-minded people like herself. Few of them would welcome some wacko who called herself a Christian.

So again, with sincere concern, Emily tried to set her friend straight, saying, "Shhhh . . . you don't know who you're lining yourself up with. And don't call God that!"

In spite of what Emily saw as Lauren's strange religious beliefs, the two women turned out to be not only regular gym associates but good friends. They saw each other at 6:00 A.M. every day, five days a week, in the women's locker room.

Bit by bit Emily poured out her soul to Lauren because Lauren listened with extreme kindness as if she really cared. Emily tried to expand their relationship to include her in other activities she and her friends took part in like political causes, downtown rallies, defending abortion clinics, or the many parties she gave. But Lauren always said no, and Emily began to understand how different they were. They talked about a lot of issues that touched both of them deeply and clearly disagreed about many things, but Lauren never became cruelly angry with Emily the way most people who disagreed with her did.

Emily continued to fight battles in the world, both in her personal and professional life. Because Lauren had great insight about life and people, Emily continued to talk with Lauren about her hurts and fears, her friends and lovers, her causes and beliefs, and her artwork and the art world. Emily watched Lauren go through struggles too, but she always seemed to trust in that God of hers.

One morning in the locker room, Lauren gave Emily a Bible. Emily was mortified. It was big and red and wouldn't fit inside her gym bag. But they'd been friends for over a year by then, so she felt she couldn't refuse this unwanted gift. Emily saw something new in Lauren that day in how much she loved that book she presented with such love and joy. In giving Emily that Bible, it was as if she was giving her a part of herself.

Of all the things Lauren told Emily, the one Emily remembered the most was hearing in no uncertain terms that God loved her. It made her cry.

"Lauren, I'm sure you believe that God of yours loves you, and I'm sure he could love you. But he could *never* love me," she said.

Over the next four years their locker room discussions continued. Emily married one of her lovers and should have been on top of the world, but she wasn't. In fact, she was just the opposite. She had a deep, dark secret: she was filled with tremendous, overwhelming fear and despair.

She couldn't stop thinking about a riddle: "What would you do if you were trapped in a room with a hungry lion and there was no way out?" "Pray, I guess," was the shrugged-out answer most people gave.

*Pray,* Emily thought. *What kind of answer is that? That's no answer!* Yet she felt trapped inside that room as if the hungry lion was life itself. She faced watching people she loved dying and herself growing older . . . all for what?

For years Emily believed an existentialist theory that goes something like this: All humans, in order to stay functional, must live in a constant state of denial. If we really perceived our reality—which is that we do not know who we are, why we are here, when we will die, or what happens to us after we die—we would go running stark raving mad in the street.

But she *did* perceive something—she didn't know any of those things. And she couldn't handle it and was finally tired of trying. She secretly wanted off this planet. Friends and family would have been shocked to have found the suicide note she wrote.

Emily expected panic when she confided the contents of her note to Lauren, but Lauren gave her a calm, steady gaze that was full of love. She asked, "Emily, would you consider coming with me to my church next Sunday?"

Emily was dumbstruck. *How in the world was going to church a solution?* She squirmed and shifted her weight, then started to speak, but nothing came out.

148

"Church?" was all she could say.

"You might like it. You just might find some of those answers you've always looked for."

Emily realized she had nowhere else to turn. She was at the end of her rope.

"Okay," was all she managed to say. They arranged to meet the following Sunday morning.

Throughout the church service, Emily felt self-conscious and out of place. Besides being uncomfortable with all the hymn singing, she couldn't understand what the people were talking about. It was like hearing a foreign language. However, during the announcements (when for a few moments it sounded like they were speaking regular English) one of the pastors described a series of classes called "Discovering Christianity" which would start the following Sunday. The description caught her attention. When she got home, she told her husband about the course.

"I don't want to go to any church service," Neil said, "but I'll check out the classes with you if you'd like."

The following week they attended "Discovering Christianity" with Lauren. The teacher explained answers to questions Emily had wondered about for years and ones she'd never thought of asking. She was amazed to hear him substantiate everything he taught with objective facts. What she was hearing was remarkable and quite possibly more important than anything she'd ever been taught before. She had never heard that Jesus was a real, historical figure who really had walked this earth and called himself God, which made him either a liar, a lunatic, or who he said he was.

Throughout the following week she thought about everything she'd heard. *Could it be, could it really possibly be?*

*Could Jesus have been God? Surely that would be impossible! If that were true, then that would mean there is a God, and that would change everything!*

The night after the second class, Emily had a dream she would never forget. In the dream she was talking on the phone with her mother, telling her she'd like to come home. To her shock, her mother interrupted her and said, "No, you cannot come home."

Emily tensed up. "What do you mean I cannot come home? I want to come home! I need to come home!"

"No, you cannot," her mother answered. "In fact, the truth is, if you do come home, your home will not be here. I will not be here. There is no home."

"What?" Emily screamed. "Don't say that!" She threw down the phone and ran outside in terror, desperate to find her home. She ran into what seemed like an endless gray mist. As she blindly raced, not knowing which way to go, she became hideously ugly, repulsive, as her skin began to fall off. She became a terrible monster. Her worst fear was death, and she was becoming death personified.

In this odious state of fear and desperation, lost in the world and lost to herself, a figure stepped out of the mist and wrapped his arms fully around her. At once she was filled with three feelings she had never known before: total peace, complete safety, and deep, incomprehensible love.

Emily gasped and sat up in bed, heart pounding and wide awake.

It was Jesus.

She looked over at her sleeping husband, who was undisturbed by her epiphany. *What do I do?* she wondered. Then she remembered something the teacher had said the day before about asking Jesus into your heart. So she said out loud but soft enough to not wake her husband, "Jesus, I know you're real. Please come into my heart, and please lock the door from the inside and don't ever, ever leave." Then she slid down under the covers and fell into the most peaceful sleep she'd ever known.

The next morning when she woke up, Jesus was on her mind, and the words "He's real!" burst out of her lips. She couldn't wait to get dressed. Her husband eyed her curiously because she was full of joy, a feeling he had never seen in her, a feeling she had never experienced. She wanted to run out into the streets and look at everything as if for the first time. She wanted to sing and shout and leap for joy.

She grabbed the big red Bible Lauren had given her four years earlier. Now she couldn't put it down.

When Emily told Lauren, she squealed with delight and immediately said, "Oh, wouldn't it be great if your husband could know Jesus too!"

"Lauren, Neil isn't like me. He's really into martial arts and Buddhism, and he's not plagued by fears like I have been."

Six weeks later Emily and Neil had taken all six classes and the first of another course on foundations of the Christian faith. One Sunday after class, Neil said he wanted to stay for church. That same night as they were getting into bed, he said, "Emily, I saw how much you changed, and it looked so good. I wasn't sure what to do, but I heard myself saying, 'Lord, I'm crazy for her. I love her so much. Lord, I think maybe you've called on her, and I want to be where she is. Would you come and get me too?'" Jesus made himself real to Neil too.

As an artist, Emily knows she can create many things, and she has a gifted imagination. But could she have imagined

Jesus? No way. Up until the moment Christ appeared in her dream, she had been repelled by his very name. After having been given a glimpse of his absolute perfection, she knows it would have been impossible for her to invent what she didn't know. Everything she knew of life was tainted with some flaw, some limitation. Until she met Jesus.

He came alongside her. He put his arms around her and revealed himself to her. Total peace, complete safety, and incomprehensible, perfect love came only from him.

Before Emily met Jesus, the first thing she did each morning was to go into her studio and slave away at her work. Now she went into the Master Artist's study, eagerly picking up God's Word and reading it for hours. It didn't make her less productive; instead, she sensed new inspiration and creativity welling up from within. She also began to reach out to others in the art world and show the love of Christ to them as Lauren had done for her. And that same Bible that had seemed like nonsense and gobbledygook became Life to her. Jesus became her refuge, for she was safely hidden in the Rock, no longer living in terror or despair.

The Bible says that perfect love drives out fear (1 John 4:18). Since Emily met Jesus, she's been through innumerable trials, but through them she's found that knowing Christ is immeasurably greater than anything else one could possibly think or imagine (Eph. 3:20), that he shines in darkness (John 1:5), and that whoever he sets free is free indeed (John 8:36).

## Catching a Fresh Vision of Jesus

"Have you seen Jesus? Then you will want others to see Him too," said Oswald Chambers in *My Utmost for His Highest*.[1]

Nothing compares to the joy of being a part of the salvation experience in a person's life. As we see a new believer's awakening, we get a fresh revelation of the power of Christ to save. Here are some things we can glean from the lives of Emily and Lauren that can help us get a fresh vision of Jesus:

*Be a stepping-stone, not a stumbling block.* With Lauren's patient listening and unconditional love, she was the stepping-stone God used to draw Emily—not overnight or in a few weeks, but through a four-year process. People around you are wrestling as Emily did with questions like "What am I doing on this earth? What's the point of life? Why should I go on living?" They may have an emptiness inside them nothing will fill except a relationship with God yet be trying to close the gap with drugs, alcohol, lovers, or immersion in the art, business, or sports world. Or they may be trying to find happiness through money or relationships. What people in your life need God? How could you be a stepping-stone for them?

*Pray out of the box.* The Lord reveals himself in many different ways: through Scripture, through the beauty of nature, through the trials we go through, and even sometimes in a dramatic way like through Emily's life-changing dream. Jesus didn't stop appearing to people after he met Paul on the road to Damascus. As Lee Strobel says in *The Case for Faith,* God still uses visions and dreams to reveal himself, not only to atheists and agnostics but also to those from other religions. In fact, Strobel says, "virtually every Muslim who has come to follow Christ has done so either because of the love of Christ expressed through a Christian or because of a vision, dream, or some other supernatural intervention."[2]

Pray for those you know who are struggling through life without a relationship with God. Don't limit how creatively

God might draw them in. Pray that the Spirit will open their eyes so they might see Jesus and "turn from darkness to light, and from the power of Satan to God. Then they will receive forgiveness for their sins and be given a place among God's people" (Acts 26:18).

SIXTEEN

# The Road
# to Emmaus

*If you wish to be disappointed, look to others.*
*If you wish to be downhearted, look to yourself.*
*If you wish to be encouraged . . . look upon Jesus*
*Christ.*

ERICH SAUER

The pair trudged down the dusty road. The seven-mile trek to Emmaus would take most of the afternoon, but the two men had so much to discuss that the time passed quickly. Oblivious to their surroundings, they were deep in conversation about the stunning events of the past week.

"I still expect to hear his voice," Cleopas said. "I would give anything to have one more chance to talk with him or listen to him teach. We should have fought back! If only we'd risen up and rescued him before it was too late. Maybe we could have done something . . ." He gazed down the road as if searching for the Master.

The other disciple nodded in agreement. "No wonder the soldiers mock us. They say his followers will drift apart now that Jesus is dead."

"*If* he is dead," Cleopas said. This sparked an intense conversation as they wrestled with what they had heard that morning. Mary Magdalene, Joanna, and Mary, the mother of James, had burst into the house, talking all at once. They had just returned from Jesus' tomb, where they had discovered that the massive rock door had been pried away. Inside they found only linens. Someone had stolen Jesus' body!

Suddenly two men in shining garments spoke to them. "Why do you look for the living among the dead?" one had asked the women. Now the women said the men were angels. But what did they know?

"Perhaps it was a dream," Cleopas said. He kicked a stone with his sandal.

His companion shook his head. "A dream? The women were not asleep! Why would they tell us this news unless they saw it with their own eyes? These are trustworthy women. Perhaps they *did* see the men. Maybe they were angels sent from God."

Cleopas laughed bitterly. "Or perhaps the soldiers hid his body," he said. "Don't fall into the trap they set. It's exactly what they are hoping we do. They want to mock us and make us appear foolish! Jesus said that he would be resurrected on the third day. They realize every eye is on that tomb right now. You can be certain they will let us know where they have placed his body—once they are ready to cause us further embarrassment."

"But what if . . ." the other disciple hesitated, creasing his brow as he stared at his friend. "Cleopas, why did Jesus say that he would rise from the tomb in three days? I remember his words distinctly. Maybe there *were* angels at the tomb. It could be that we just didn't listen. Who are the foolish ones then?"

Cleopas shrugged. "Jesus is dead." He hung his head, staring at the dust swirling around his sandals. "I saw them put his body in the tomb."

They walked slowly as they continued their debate. Suddenly a stranger came alongside and joined them as they continued their journey. Cleopas stared at the man and frowned. "We must have been so deep in conversation we didn't see you behind us," he said.

The man said to them, "What are you talking about as you walk along?" The men stood looking at the stranger, their faces crestfallen with sadness and disappointment.

"Are you the only one in Jerusalem who hasn't heard what's happened during the last few days?" Cleopas asked.

The man replied, "What happened?"

Both men tried to explain. It was difficult to put it into words and even more difficult to make it clear to a man who had no inkling of the wild and tragic events. One of the men threw his hands up in the air. "We must start at the beginning," he said. "Jesus the Nazarene was a man of God. We believed in him. He was a prophet who did miracles and taught truths we'd never heard. He was blessed by both God

157

and all the people. Then our high priests and leaders betrayed him and had him sentenced to death and crucified. We had our hopes up that he was the Messiah who would deliver Israel. We thought he would throw off the oppression of the Romans and set up a great kingdom. Now all is lost. Today is the third day since it happened."

Cleopas jumped into the conversation. "Some of our women have astounded us. Early this morning they went to the tomb and his body was gone! They came back and told us that they had seen angels who said Jesus was alive. Some of our friends went off to the tomb to check, and it was empty just as the women said. But they didn't see Jesus, and they doubt the women's story."

The stranger stopped in the middle of the road. "So thick-headed! So slow-hearted! Why can't you simply believe all that the prophets said? Don't you see that these things had to happen, that the Messiah had to suffer and only then enter into his glory?"

The two men weren't sure how to respond. Maybe this was a teacher of the Law. In any case, the stranger fell into step beside them as they continued walking on the dusty road.

"Let's start with Moses," he said. As they walked the men listened eagerly as he explained the Scriptures in fresh new ways, discussed the prophets, and pointed out references to the death and resurrection of the Messiah.

The sounds from the village reminded the men that Emmaus lay directly ahead. Children called out in play, and the smell of fish cooking over coals wafted through the air. When the man turned as if he was leaving them, Cleopas called out to him, "Please, stay and eat supper with us. It's nearly evening." So he went on into Emmaus with them.

They pushed through the city streets, greeting those who recognized them but eager to resume their discussion. When they reached the house, Cleopas started to introduce the stranger to his friends but realized he did not even know who the man was. Cleopas laughed, clapping his hands together. "We've been talking about the Messiah so much I didn't even ask your name," he said.

The man smiled. "Come, let us wash our feet, and then we will eat."

They sat at the table and the stranger picked up the bread, blessed it, and broke it. Then he gave the bread to them, saying, "Peace be to you." As the crumbs fell to the table, the two men stared. Their eyes were suddenly opened, and they recognized the stranger as the light dawned in their hearts.

"Jesus?" Cleopas said. "Can it be you, my Lord?" He pushed aside his food, leaped up from the table, and danced around the room in joy as he made his way to his Messiah. The other disciple leaned over to clasp Jesus' hand when suddenly he disappeared.

"How could we not have recognized him?" They talked back and forth excitedly, trying to explain what had happened. "Didn't we feel on fire as he conversed with us on the road, as he opened up the Scriptures for us?" they said. "We must find him!"

As they ran out the door, the men felt like their souls were lit with flames. It didn't matter that the sun was setting. They didn't care that they were hungry and tired. They had seen the Savior! They had good news to share, and they didn't want to waste one more minute. Waving good-bye to their stunned friends, they hurried down the road. They had to get to Jerusalem to tell the disciples what had happened. Cleopas leaped in the air as they ran, shouting, not caring who heard him, letting all who would listen hear the good news. "He's alive!" he said, throwing his head back and laughing with joy. "Jesus is alive!"

Before long they found the eleven disciples and their friends huddled together behind locked doors in Jerusalem, cowering in fear of what the Jewish leaders might do next.

"The Lord has risen! It's really happened!" Cleopas and the other disciple shouted as they rushed into the room. They told all about their experiences on the road and how they recognized Jesus in the breaking of the bread.[1]

## Catching a Fresh Vision of Jesus

When Jesus met the two disciples on the road, they were long-faced and defeated. They hadn't waited for him in Galilee as the angel had instructed. Some of his followers had gone home. Most of the disciples hid in a room in Jerusalem behind a locked door because of their fear and despair. Cleopas and his companion had set out on the road to Emmaus. Yet Jesus showed up and walked along beside the two men. He showed up in the locked room and revealed himself to his followers. And he is still showing up for you and me. We can catch a fresh revelation of him when we realize:

*He's alive and in our midst.* Perhaps you, like the two men on the dusty road to Emmaus, know what it's like to lose heart. To feel like everything has failed. To know your human efforts are exhausted and you're at the end of your rope. This story shows us that when we are most helpless, when the circumstances look impossible and we feel most discouraged, Jesus is there. When every door has closed in our career, when our marriage seems most lifeless or our teenager most incorrigible, Christ is in our midst. He comes alongside us in our distress just as he came alongside the downcast disciples—and he specializes in resurrections.

Too often, however, we are unaware of his presence because we're so absorbed in our pain. Like Cleopas and his friend, who looked so intently at the dust on the ground that they didn't notice the risen King standing beside them, we don't notice his love or blessings. We forget the promises he has given us in the Scriptures and can only see the dreadful circumstances. But still Jesus graciously comes and meets us wherever we are, even in our pain or discouragement.

When we look to ourselves, we'll continue to be down-hearted and in despair. When we look to others to save us, we will ultimately be disappointed at their failure. But when we look to Jesus, our hearts will be strangely warmed and renewed, just as the two men from Emmaus experienced.

*Experience Christ through communion.* Jesus revealed himself in the intimate moments when he broke the bread, blessed it, and gave it to the two men in Emmaus, and he invites us to draw near to him at the communion table in the same way. He invites us to take the grape juice and bread not as an empty ritual or just to remember back to an event two thousand years ago but in expectation of the presence of Jesus in our own lives and in the church where we fellowship. Communion is much more than revisiting a historical event. It's an opportunity for connection and intimacy with our Savior. Therefore we are to come expectantly and reverently, with prepared hearts that forgive, worship, and praise.

As Paul said, "Examine your motives, test your heart, come to this meal in holy awe" (1 Cor. 11:28 MESSAGE). The next time you prepare to take communion, ask yourself, *What would I do if Christ's literal presence entered the room? How would I prepare myself to meet with him?*

Then you can "feed on Christ," as Phillips Brooks said, "and then go and live your life, and it is Christ in you that lives your life, that helps the poor, that tells the truth, that fights the battle, and that wins the crown."[2]

# SEVENTEEN

# The Trysting Place

*When we meet the Christ, the living Christ, we come to life again. With faith that springs from the depth of our joy, we run to the trash cans to retrieve the dreams and hopes we'd thrown away in our despair. Eagerly we pull them out, dust them off, and find to our joyful amazement that they are not only still intact, they are gloriously enhanced. . . . And we turn to Christ with a new light in our eyes, showing him our dreams in a speechless thankfulness.*

JIM MCGUIGGAN
*JESUS, HERO OF THY SOUL*

Have you noticed the way the world stops at the instant of a great loss, freeze-framing the colors, sights, and sounds around you? All these years later I remember being in gym class and hearing the *click* and *squawk* of the public address system that foreshadowed the announcement that would forever change America: *"President Kennedy has been assassinated."*

We all suffer those collective sorrows, like the moment the space shuttle *Challenger* broke apart. I watched the coverage, willing the astronauts to have survived the blast, willing a billowing parachute to appear. We remember other moments: the bombing of the Oklahoma City federal building, Princess Diana's death, the attacks on the World Trade Center and the Pentagon.

It was that kind of moment when Flo Perkins died.

Who was Flo? She never met a president. She wasn't an astronaut. Her death wasn't broadcast on the television news. But in a tiny stucco house in Oklahoma, Flo Perkins led a heroic life.

West Texas, 1926. A west wind blew up dust in the streets of a small Texas town as ten-year-old Floria hurried to the restaurant where she worked. Her dark braid swayed as she stepped onto a milk crate to dry and sort the silverware. Hazel eyes shining, she watched the people who came to the restaurant to eat. The women wore elegant dresses and bright red nail polish. The men wore suits and felt hats. Children wriggled in their chairs, hardly noticing the fine food set before them.

Floria sighed, leaning against the oak breakfront that held the silverware. Closing her eyes, she tried to imagine wearing fine clothes and sitting in a restaurant to eat. Then she picked up a knife and polished it until she could see her reflection in the handle. In the dining room a man with dark brown hair laughed at the antics of his daughter. Floria stopped. *That must be what my daddy is like.*

Truth be told, she didn't have a thimbleful of information about her father. Born in Oklahoma in 1916, Floria had been four years old when her parents divorced. Since then she and her mother moved from state to state, from town to dusty town, from one restaurant to the next, with people of every size and shape weaving in and out of the picture.

After work Floria hurried back to the dismal boarding house where her mother rented a room, and she fell into the sagging bed. She was exhausted, and not just from working long hours to help pay the rent and put food on the table. She was exhausted from the constant moving, never staying long enough to make friends before her mom shuffled her off to chase after some new rainbow. *Not that I'd have time to play with a friend if I had one,* Flo thought as she stared at the cracked ceiling.

It was longing more than labor that wearied her. Sometimes she ached with desire for something . . . *normal.* She would love to be surrounded with the same things, the same faces, and the same scenery every day. It wouldn't have to be anything fancy, like fine two-story houses or shiny new Model A motor cars.

Ten-year-old Floria hungered to come home to the same front door every night. To sit at the same kitchen table and eat from familiar dishes. To have her mom knitting by a fire and her father dozing over the newspaper. On the rare occasions that Flo got to go to school, she labored over her penmanship in hopes that some day she could write her father a letter. *But where would I send it?* she thought. *I don't even know where he lives.*

Sundays were the worst—days when the church bells tolled and families strolled inside, arm in arm. Flo had never been inside a church and had no idea why people went. She only knew that deep inside her grew a yearning to be part of a family.

Flo let her mind travel back to the little mining town in Utah where she and her mother had lived for a while at the foot of snow-covered mountains. She could still smell the crisp, clean morning air and see the majesty of the mountains. That town had been the hardest one to leave, but her heart had found comfort in the stars over the desert as they drove along harrowing roads in stifling heat. In one Texas town she'd been assigned to an exceptional teacher who sparked a love of books and helped Flo learn to read.

Flo heard the creaking stairs before her mother let herself into the room. "You still awake?" her mother asked.

"Yes, ma'am."

"You might as well get up and help me pack. I heard there's work in West Texas."

Flo showed no expression as she pulled her bedraggled bag from below the bed.

In December 1928 they landed in Oklahoma City. Tall for her age, Flo looked a lot older than twelve. "No more school for you," her mother informed her. "We need money to survive, and you've got to help earn it."

Flo had to lie about her age to earn a dollar a day washing dishes. Two years later, at age fourteen, she got a job at Kress, a large department store in downtown Oklahoma City. Her employer thought she was eighteen. While doing inventory one day, a woman working alongside Flo described the great love of her life—Jesus. Flo listened intently as the woman described Jesus as her Bridegroom. Flo's fertile imagination captured the image and wondered how God could come as Son and husband.

Intrigued with Jesus, Flo borrowed a Bible to read about him, but she couldn't understand the words. That night she heard singing outside her rooming house window. Ever curious, she searched out the source of the sound. The music came from a small mission not far from where she lived. No church bell was tolling and Flo had no family surrounding her, but she went to the mission anyway.

The following Sunday she attended a meeting at the mission and met a young man named Oscar Perkins. Oscar walked her home and described his conversion experience. A week later he asked her to marry him.

Like everyone else, Oscar thought Flo was older. She had no idea what love was, but Oscar seemed a gentle man, and she was hungry for a family of her own. On August 17, 1930, fourteen-year-old Flo donned her Sunday best and stood before the justice of the peace to say her vows to Oscar.

It was the second year of the Great Depression, and Oscar and Flo were dirt poor and in good company. They had no wedding cake or fancy reception, no honeymoon or bridal shower. But it was the best day of young Flo's life.

Life was simple. The way she understood it, Jesus brought her a husband. Because of Jesus she would never have to be alone again. The same day Flo said "I do" to Oscar, she bowed her heart before the Judge of heaven and said "I do" to Jesus with a heart filled with gratitude. In one day she became bride to two bridegrooms.

She'd learned enough at the mission to know that when she made that vow to Jesus, she was transferred from the darkness of her past to the light and newness of life. She read in 2 Corinthians 5:17 that when a person comes to Christ, she becomes a new person. Flo laid everything—her past and her future—on the altar before Jesus and sensed a fullness she'd never known in her fourteen lonely years.

Flo knew very little about Christian living but was thrilled when Oscar taught her from the Bible. They lived by the river in a shack that often flooded. But it was *their* shack, and Flo never grumbled or complained. Even though she worked long days, she rose early every morning to give praise to God.

Eventually Oscar bought a small plot of land as far from the flood zone as he could. There he built a tiny three-room stucco home with an outhouse. *A house of our own!* thought Flo. *I'll enter the same front door every evening! I'll put food on the same kitchen table!* Overcome with joy, she poured out her adoration to Jesus.

In that house Oscar and Flo raised four children and later several grandchildren. Flo helped them with their homework by lamplight each night as Oscar dozed. Years later Oscar added a bathroom and an extra bedroom and converted the original kitchen into a dining room.

Every morning at 5:30 Flo knelt at the east window, which she called her "trysting place," and met the Bridegroom of her heart. A trysting place, Flo once told me, was an appointed meeting place for lovers, and Jesus was truly the lover of her soul. She drank in his presence and found a refuge for her soul. She found someone who listened as she poured out to him the burdens of raising four children and Oscar's long battle with cancer. In Jesus she found stability and joy during every season of her life. He was her source of sanity when life seemed out of control. He was there to run to when Oscar breathed his last.

As Flo launched her days from the trysting place, the little gray stucco house became a veritable lighthouse. Granting Flo the greatest desire of her heart—a familiar place to awaken every morning—God allowed her to minister to generations of neighborhood children during her fifty years in the home that love built. She fed the children wisdom along with cookies, crackers, and popsicles. The neighborhood was rough, and many of the families were as transient as hers had been. She understood the hunger of their hearts, and they recognized it. Along with blankets, sacks of groceries, and money, Flo gave to needy people she met life-sustaining prayer, Bibles, and the greatest gift of all—Jesus.

But more than anything, Flo prayed in her trysting place. She prayed for every girl and boy who lived in her neighborhood and continued to pray for them after they moved away from the neighborhood and out of childhood. Young people from around the city converted in the Jesus Movement of the '70s made their way to her door and found wisdom. She taught Sunday school and taught others how to do what she did daily for sixty years—go into the presence of Jesus and talk with him.

Flo taught me to pray. Prayer was as easy as breathing for her. She prayed for my children's broken bones and wounded hearts. Her prayers sustained me when my mother died. She prayed for my writing career and paved the way in the heavenlies for all the books I would write. Her little stucco home was a refuge for so many. And her trysting place was the place from which my own prayer life was launched.

That's why the news of Flo Perkins's death is forever frozen in my memory alongside the deaths of presidents, astronauts, and royalty. On the cold December day of her funeral, I gathered with family and friends next to her trysting place. We sang and shared what she'd meant in our lives. I was stunned at the impact she'd had on so many lives. She had gained no fame or fortune on earth, but I knew beyond a doubt that all of heaven rejoiced at her homecoming.

Today Flo Perkins is reunited with both of her bridegrooms—Jesus and Oscar. She has a home of her own for all of eternity. Her trysting place is face to face.

## Catching a Fresh Vision of Jesus

Like Flo, we all need a daily trysting time with Jesus to walk God's pathway consistently through each season and challenge of life. Her life reminds me of Psalm 25:4–5: "Show me your ways, O LORD, teach me your paths; guide me in your truth and teach me, for you are God my Savior, and my hope is in you all day long" (NIV). Here are some ways to apply this to your life:

*Start the day with Jesus.* Naval officers used to keep their ships on course on ocean journeys by securing a "celestial fix" on the stars. By fixing on the first stars of the evening and the last stars before daylight, they navigated steadily and made any course correction necessary.[1]

If we aren't fixing our minds on Jesus and seeking him daily, we can easily drift and fall back into old ways instead of walking in newness of life. But if we set our hearts, as Flo did, on being with our Bridegroom and having our own "celestial fix," we can experience his presence all day long. When or where you have your trysting place isn't the main thing; what's important is that you set your heart to seek the Lord so the tyranny of the urgent won't take away your precious time with him.

*Be transformed.* Flo Perkins experienced a dramatic transformation when she said yes to Jesus and he brought her out of a life of spiritual poverty to lasting, eternal riches. That transformation didn't happen overnight; it occurred day by day as she walked with him through life.

For each of us as well, the real test of a newfound faith is transformation. "Faith in Jesus, real faith—accepting Him in all of His Deity, a full surrender to Him produces an incredible change—a transformation of the whole person," says Jim Craddock, founder of Scope Ministries. "Faith without surrender is a life without living. Christians, who come face to face with the indisputable fact that Jesus does indeed have a claim upon their lives, are permanently, indelibly transformed."[2]

Do you have an insatiable desire to know Christ and his book, the Bible? Are you being transformed by walking and talking with him throughout your daily life? Write a prayer expressing your heart's desire to know the Lord, and if your love for him has grown cold or been diminished by the cares and busyness of your life, ask him to stir up your hunger and thirst to really "know Christ and experience the mighty power that raised him from the dead" (Phil. 3:10).

# PART 5

# A Fresh Vision
*of* Jesus through
His Whispers

# EIGHTEEN

# The Lord Our Reconciler

*Reconciliation is not weakness or cowardice. It demands courage, nobility, generosity, sometimes heroism, an overcoming of oneself rather than of one's adversary.*

POPE PAUL VI

As I sat on the jet about to take off from Will Rogers World Airport in Oklahoma City, I gazed out the window at Holmes and our three children waving good-bye from the gate. The next morning my mother was having a lung biopsy to determine whether she had cancer or not. We hoped with all our hearts for the latter outcome.

Only fifty-nine years old, Mom was vibrant and active and enjoyed every day at her east Texas ranch. Just a few days before, she'd finished planting her garden and pruned her beloved pear trees in the backyard. She relished spending time with her brood, traveling, and cooking for family and friends. But a persistent cough had drained her energy for months and caused respiratory infections. After trying numerous medications, her internist felt they had to do a biopsy to rule out cancer.

"Pray that whatever it is, God will heal me," Mom had asked on the phone the day before.

"Sure, Mom, we've been praying for you every day and will keep it up. I'll see you as soon as I can get to the hospital."

I looked out the window as I asked God to give the doctors wisdom and to strengthen Mom and restore her health. When I finished my litany of requests and sat silently, I heard the Spirit say, "It's the sunset of your mother's life. Be there beside her. Don't be in denial."

*Naturally I want to be there for her. Mama was always there for me*, I silently responded, my mind going back to all the times we'd shared. Every birthday, every sickness, after school . . . Mom was there. She took us to church and smiled from the audience at every talent show, drill team parade, and graduation. She was there to organize my wedding and help me after the birth of each of my babies. *Of course I want to be there for Mom. But by "sunset" surely you mean in the last years of her life, Lord.*

"No, she is in the sunset of her life *now*," I heard.

This was *not* what I'd hoped to hear after praying for Mom on the eve of her surgery. I'd thought she could surely bounce back from this illness. *You could do this, Lord! Healing Mama would be no big deal for you. And she has so much more she wants to get done on earth before she goes home. Couldn't you give her some more years like you gave Hezekiah? And please help her recover from this surgery quickly.*

"I know you want your mother to get well, but I have a different prayer assignment for you," I sensed the Lord's quiet whisper saying. "I want you to pray for reconciliation between your sister Martha and your mom before she goes to heaven."

"Before she goes to heaven?" I gulped. That sounded far too imminent and final. My heart sunk, and tears slipped down my cheeks because I couldn't even fathom the possibility of life without Mom. Since my father had died at age forty-seven, Mom was both mother love and father love to all of us. She was the matriarch of our big Heath clan, the gatherer of her six children, their spouses, and twenty grandchildren for big cookouts and holidays at her Texas ranch.

But the instructions were clear. Somehow I was to shift my prayer focus from the healing of a body to the healing of a relationship.

Reconciliation. Now *that* would be a miracle. Although they loved each other, Martha and Mama had a stormy relationship as far back as I could remember. Whenever they were together they seemed to hurt each other, and Martha couldn't get past the past.

I prayed, *Lord, thank you for guiding me to pray for reconciliation, because it must be your plan, but this is really hard. Help me to release Mom and keep my eyes on you, trusting you to work and bring forgiveness to both of their hearts.*

The next morning following surgery we got the verdict: a virulent cancer had spread from an unknown organ and now was afflicting her lungs. She had one to six months to live, the doctor said.

"Can't you do chemotherapy? Radiation? Surely there's something you can do to stop the growth of the cancer," we questioned.

"At this point, it's just not going to help," the doctor answered. "If we'd found it in the early stages, things would have been different, but it's too late. We can try some radiation treatments to slow the cancer before it spreads to the brain, but I'm not optimistic about the outcome."

*Too late? It's never too late for God.* We rallied as a family and redoubled our prayers on Mom's behalf. Her church and other churches prayed. Her pastor came to the hospital room and prayed for her many times. Scores of friends came to visit and said, "Get well soon!" adding their prayers to the mass of intercession going up to heaven on Mom's behalf. God heard her name over and over.

And every day I kept praying for reconciliation between Martha and Mom: *Lord, fill them with forgiveness. Bridge the gap between them and soften their hearts. Restore their relationship and bring them to reconciliation.*

I got my hopes up when I heard Martha was coming into town to see Mama again. As I saw her coming down the hall a few days later, I thought, *This is the day.* But when she left to go back to Houston twenty-four hours later, there was no sign of peace between these two strong-willed people I loved. My heart plummeted.

*Lord, you know I'm discouraged. Give me the faith to keep praying and believing that you are able to do this.*

Martha's second visit, when we all gathered for the Fourth of July at the ranch, was no better. By the end of the weekend, that big unseen grudge hadn't moved an inch.

And in spite of radiation treatments at Baylor Hospital, alternative treatment in another state, and many vitamins, my mother's health went steadily downhill. By early September, only four months after the diagnosis, the doctor informed us that she had only a few weeks to live. Time was running out.

Oh, how much lies behind the scenes that we who see through a glass darkly don't perceive! What I didn't know was that before Martha came back to Dallas to visit Mom for the last time, God had been at work in her heart. For a long time she'd been aware of how deeply bitter she was at Mama. But Martha wouldn't—or couldn't—do anything about it. She resented Mama's "religiosity," as she called it, and felt that Mama ought to finally say to her, "Okay, I failed you in this area and that area," but the apologies never came. Mama felt her second-born daughter was hard-headed, and Martha felt constantly criticized instead of supported.

At the same time, Martha was slowly and surely dying of alcoholism the same way our uncle had. She had no success in staying sober. She had been around Alcoholics Anonymous for several years, yet had never worked all twelve steps. Lately, however, that word "forgiveness" seemed to crop up wherever she went. For example, one day Martha's sponsor listened to her fifth step: admitting to God, to herself, and to someone else the exact nature of her wrongs. As Martha finished the step and walked out the door, the woman spoke one word: *forgiveness.* "Martha, *forgiveness,*" she seemed almost to be begging.

So as Martha drove the several hundred miles from her home to the hospital for the last time, she intended to finally find a way to forgive. She had the desire to forgive and the knowledge that she needed to do it. But what became increasingly clear was that she didn't have *the capacity* to forgive.

179

"In my heart of hearts," she confided to me in the hall outside Mama's room the night she arrived, "I want to forgive her, but I can't get rid of the poison of bitterness I've carried my whole life. The more I try, the more I realize it's going to take God to do that. I don't just need a little help from God. I need God to give me the forgiveness I need for Mom."

That very night Mama went into a coma, so now the reconciliation looked even more impossible. I knew that in the weeks before, Mama had had lots of talks with God, repenting for many things, even as small as a bad attitude toward a difficult neighbor. She'd asked forgiveness for everything and forgiven everyone he brought to mind, including her daughter Martha. But now that they couldn't even talk, how could Martha come to peace with her?

For three nights in a row, the doctor told us, "This will probably be the night she'll die. Her lungs and heart just don't have the capacity to keep on functioning." But somehow, she held on. As she did, Martha's confidence grew that somehow she'd get that forgiveness before her mother died.

For the third night's vigil, all five of us sisters were around Mom's bed. By 2:00 A.M. all of us except Martha had dozed off, exhausted from the long nights at the hospital. Wide awake in the dark room, she knelt at the head of Mom's bed and held her hand. The idea came to her to let God go with her through the pages of her life, through every single thing that had bugged her about Mom, every unfair punishment and every perceived wrongdoing. She would ask God to enable her to forgive Mom for each and every one of those things, because she knew surely she couldn't do that.

She knelt on a pillow on the cold hospital floor. Holding Mama's wrist and feeling her pulse grow weaker by the moment, Martha and the Lord together marched back through those ugly times, through pages and pages of the vignettes of her life: the time she was punished by not getting to go to her Sunday school picnic; times she was spanked and felt she didn't deserve it; all the times she'd felt denied the love she longed for.

As the Spirit brought each hurtful experience onto the movie screen of her mind, she said, "Lord, forgive this for me." For the next memory and the next she prayed, "Let your forgiveness flow through me for this." And so on she went through the memories of her childhood and teenage years until, at the very moment Mom's pulse ceased to beat, every hurt was forgiven. As Martha's life had passed before her, each resentment against Mom had been released. That gnarled-up knot in the middle of her being was gone, and a sense of relief washed over her. God had done for her what she couldn't do for herself: forgive.

Just at that moment of death and release, as the rest of us slept, Martha saw the indescribable presence of angels around the bed tenderly attending Mama and escorting her soul as it soared heavenward. What a great gift that was.

But even greater than seeing the angels was that with the chains of bitterness broken off, she gained the ability to see and remember all the good things in her childhood like the happy times with Mama and Papa, picnicking at White Rock Lake, and ice cream outings as a family. Wonderful memories flooded her mind: Mama sitting at her pedal-driven Singer machine sewing beautiful dresses for her five little daughters; the story of how Mom climbed out of the muck of Great Depression poverty and her tough Houston upbringing with her Scarlett O'Hara determination; Mama cooking big dinners; and even the delicious taste of Mama's food. And when the scales of unforgiveness fell from Martha's eyes, she was also able to see the goodness and faithfulness of God for the first time in years.

The next morning when the sun came up, God's Spirit spoke to my heart, "She has fought a good fight, she has finished the race . . . and now the prize awaits her—the crown of righteousness that the Lord, the righteous Judge, will give her on that great day of his return" (see 2 Tim. 4:7–8).

Mama was *home.* I would always miss her, but knowing that she was now in heaven seeing Jesus face to face like she'd told me she would and knowing that my sister was free from bitterness brought a great deal of comfort in the midst of my sorrow.

Forgiveness began to reshape my sister's life in the years ahead and became the doorway to her recovery from alcoholism. With the exception of one misstep a year later, she has stayed sober one day at a time, by the grace of God, for over twenty years. In the process she has held out her hand to a phenomenal number of women bound by their own addiction to alcohol and their own bitterness and pain. By sharing her experience of God's power and forgiveness again and again, she has helped many walk not only through the Twelve Steps to freedom but also into the arms of Jesus.

## Catching a Fresh Vision of Jesus

As I heard my sister share how God had brought forgiveness on the night of our mother's death, I saw Jesus in a whole new way—as the Reconciler. I had wanted him to heal Mom's body, but he knew the greater needs of the heart. Mom received the ultimate healing in heaven, and Martha received a profound healing in her soul. She had other struggles but no longer was ensnared by unforgiveness and bitterness.

I saw a glimpse of how deeply the Lord cares about the relationships in our families on this earth and how the forgiveness of sin accomplished by Jesus on the cross is meant to reconcile us not only to the Father but also to one another. He himself is our peace, Scripture says, and he breaks down the barrier of the dividing wall of hostility that stands between us in our most difficult relationships (see Eph. 2:14–16). His forgiveness provides a way to restore the days that have been destroyed through all the misunderstandings, the failures, and the hurtful things we humans do and say to one another. He came to turn the hearts of sons to their fathers (Mal. 4:6) and the hearts of daughters to their mothers and to set us free from bitterness and resentment to be free to love as he loved us. Here's how we see this aspect of Christ:

*Be a reconciler.* The word *reconciliation* means to restore to harmony, communion, or friendship. Jesus has given us, his children, the ministry of reconciliation (2 Cor. 5:18), and the fundamental way we can be a part of his reconciliation process is by praying. In prayer we lay down the tracks so God's power can come into every relationship. Do you have a broken relationship in your life? Do you know someone who needs freedom from unforgiveness or bitterness? Ask God how he wants you to pray and to clarify and shed his light on the problem or relationship.

*Get alone with God to go through the pages of your life story.* As you spend some time with the Lord, reflect on hurtful experiences and the people who caused them. Commit them to him one by one and ask him to heal those relationships and wounds that are beyond your ability to fix. As you do, you can call on the Lord our Reconciler to bring you into forgiveness and restore broken relationships. Perhaps you, like Martha, have seethed with resentment because you were wronged. Maybe your mother or another person hurt you or neglected to meet your needs. Hanging on to unforgiveness will rob you of peace, joy, and most of all freedom. But forgiveness can transform your life as it did my sister's. The root word of *forgiveness* is the Greek word for *grace,* and we experience the grace Christ offers when we turn to him and make the choice to forgive. His grace blended with love brings cleansing and wholeness to our lives.

NINETEEN

# Can You Hear
# My Voice?

*No creature has meaning without the word of God.*
*God's word is in all creation, visible and invisible.*
*The word is living, being, spirit, all verdant greening,*
*    all creativity.*
*This word flashes out in every creature.*
*This is how the spirit is in the flesh—the Word is*
*    indivisible from God.*

HILDEGARD OF BINGEN

The faint light of dawn awakened twenty-year-old Earl from his shallow slumber in a hammock hanging between two trees. It was the fifth month of his tour of duty in Vietnam. Since most of their time was spent in the bush, he and the other soldiers were accosted by leeches, snakes, scorpions, intense heat, and stifling humidity as well as enemy soldiers. Despite the ravages of the conflict he'd been thrown into, he saw evidence of the hand of the God who had created the denseness and variety of the jungle and prayed softly to him to begin the day.

Carrying their ninety-pound packs of gear, Earl's platoon set out from ChuLai to begin their search-and-destroy mission for the day. They moved swiftly through their designated area of operation, sending out patrols along the way as they looked for Vietcong.

Not far down the jungle trail, Earl noticed a pair of large green dragonflies locked in an embrace that would ensure the survival of the species at least for the foreseeable future. He wouldn't have thought they were significant, but everywhere he saw pairs of living things. Two birds flying together. Two butterflies flitting over his head. Two snakes wrapped around a tree on the path. The entire day passed with pairs cropping up around him until at last the platoon stopped to set up camp for the night.

The camp was situated on a hilltop covered with ten-foot-high elephant grass and no prominent features but two trees at the north end. After setting up his hooch, Earl pulled out his Bible and asked, "Lord, are you trying to show me something?" His eyes fell on Ecclesiastes 4:9–12:

> Two are better than one,
> because they have a good return for their work:
> If one falls down,
> his friend can help him up.
> But pity the man who falls
> and has no one to help him up!
> Also, if two lie down together, they will keep warm.
> But how can one keep warm alone?

Though one may be overpowered,
two can defend themselves.
A cord of three strands is not quickly broken.

NIV

"What are you telling me?" Earl asked the Lord. "I've already pledged myself to celibacy so I can have a significant ministry and serve you after my release from the army. So this 'twosome' idea can't apply to me. I can be much more effective in evangelism as a single."

"I'm not concerned about *your* plans, nor with what great things you hope to do for me," the voice of the Spirit interrupted. "My goal is to change your *heart* so that I can express my own life through you. The only way I can accomplish this heart-changing task in you is through the experiences of being a husband and father."

Suddenly the face of Peggy, a friend Earl had grown up with, came into his mind. *Surely I've just been in the jungle too long,* he thought.

The next day as they tramped through the jungle, Earl couldn't get Peggy or the things God had spoken out of his mind. That evening while eating a dinner of C rations, Earl was called by the platoon leader.

"Stewart! We've received a radio message that a helicopter is on its way to pick you up. The Red Cross has arranged an emergency leave for you because your father is in critical condition in a hospital back in Oklahoma."

Earl had barely packed his gear when the *whop, whop, whop* of the chopper's blades beat the thick jungle air as it settled in a small clearing. He jumped into the helicopter and sat on the edge, legs hanging, his rucksack providing the ballast to keep him from falling out. They lifted off without delay, and the other soldiers returned Earl's waves with obvious envy as the helicopter sped out of sight.

*Maybe I'll never see this place again.*

Within twenty-four hours he was back in Oklahoma City, in the intensive care unit at Baptist Hospital to see his dad, who'd suffered a near-fatal stroke. They spoke for only a few moments, but his dad asked for two matches. When Earl returned with them, he watched with amazement as his father made a cross out of the small wooden sticks; it was in essence his way of saying, "I believe." A short while later he slipped into a coma. Six days later Earl stood by the bed as his father took his last, fleeting breath.

Several friends were also at the hospital during the vigil. One of them was Peggy, the young woman Earl had seen so vividly in his mind's eye only days before. She'd had a crush on Earl since high school but had been drawn into intense intercession for him during his recent months in Vietnam. When she had learned from Earl before he left of his commitment to God as his first and only love and of his intention not to marry, Peggy placed her love for Earl on the altar and made a commitment that God himself would be her only love.

Yet as Peggy's intercession for Earl grew stronger over time, God gradually showed her that he intended to bring the two together. She kept this knowledge as a sacred secret for over a year while she continued her studies at the University of Texas.

At the very moment she was telling her dad that she wasn't returning to college but instead staying in Oklahoma City to await Earl's return, regardless of how long it took, they had received a call saying that the Red Cross was bringing Earl home because of his father's stroke.

Now Earl's dad's body had been taken to the funeral home, and Earl and Peggy sat across from each other in his living room. "There's something I've got to share with you, Peggy."

"Me too," she said.

"You go first," Earl urged.

Feeling vulnerable, Peggy opened up. "I've prayed for you ever since we became Christians. And recently the Lord showed me that it's his purpose to bring us together."

What Peggy had to say would have fallen on deaf ears had Earl not had his experience praying in the jungle. Instead he felt heartened and began to share what God had spoken to him.

"Well, let's commit ourselves to the Lord together," he suggested after they talked. They knelt down in front of the couch and prayed, "Father, we don't understand exactly what you're doing here, but it's clear you've brought us together at this time. We give ourselves to you and to each other so that your will might be accomplished in our lives. Lead us in the days to come and make of us what you would for your glory."

For the next two weeks they spent most of their waking hours together, hiking through the woods, praying, sharing Scriptures, and falling thoroughly in love. But before long came the end of February and Earl's mandatory return to Vietnam. Having to say good-bye and leave behind a love like he'd never known was the most difficult thing he'd ever done. But before he knew it, he found himself back in the jungle of Southeast Asia.

Soon a letter arrived from Peggy, but he mistakenly read it as a rejection. With the misunderstanding and lack of contact, the emotions of love he'd experienced seemed to evaporate almost as fast as they'd materialized. He cast the whole relationship back on God and began to look in Scripture to discover what real love is.

When other soldiers took cigarette breaks during their jungle missions, Earl took out his serviceman's pocket Bible. While he dug in God's Word for truth, Peggy was fervently praying for him across the ocean. Earl tramped through the bush and performed his duties every day, but his mind was constantly thinking of the verses he'd read at night and on breaks. As he read the book of Genesis, he discovered that the basis of Adam and Eve's love was the fact that they were literally a part of one another, since Eve had come from Adam's very being. He arrived at the conclusion that love is that invisible attraction, like gravity, that draws back together as one those things that were originally one.

Then he looked at the love between the Father and the Son to test out this idea, and John 17:22–23 came to mind: "I have given them the glory you gave me, so that they may be one, as we are—I in them and you in me, all being perfected into one."

*Jesus is saying the Father is in him and he is in the Father—the love of the Father and the Son existed because they were a part of one another to begin with,* Earl thought. *God loved his Son long before there was a world. Well, that can't apply to us because God's up there and we're down here; we're the creatures and he's the Creator.*

But then he read Ephesians 5:31–32: "For this cause a man shall leave his father and mother, and shall cleave to his wife; and the two shall become one flesh. This mystery is great; but I am speaking with reference to Christ and the church." *That's it!* Earl thought. *We are Christ's bride and thus a part of God through Jesus' very presence abiding in us by his Spirit.* He felt that the love he had experienced for Peggy was because they were a part of one another, meant to be husband and wife.

As the days wore on and the danger to American forces increased, Earl's platoon was threatened by death on every side. But in the midst of the battles, Earl was aware of Christ's presence with him. Before long another letter arrived from Peggy which let him know her heart was fully his.

He returned safely to Oklahoma City after his tour of duty in Vietnam and married his sweetheart. Together they have raised five children. They served as missionaries in Germany and Switzerland and have ministered to countless people during their thirty-one years of marriage.

## Catching a Fresh Vision of Jesus

A key element in our Christian lives that we often lack is understanding the principle that God's love and his relationship with us aren't based on *our performance* but on the fact that having been born of his Spirit, *we are a part of him.* As George MacDonald once said, "God is all in all, and he made us out of himself."[1] What often escapes us is the reality of the relationship we have already been given in and through Christ. As we come to grips with that relationship as Earl did in Vietnam, our life with Jesus undergoes a transformation. Life is no longer a series of attempts to appease a distant God. Rather, we see our Maker, who is our Husband, working in all things to express his love to us and to draw us into a growing intimacy with himself. His love for us is based *not* on our personal worth but on the reality that we are one with him through his Spirit. It's no longer our efforts to serve a distant God but that he whom we belong to and are a part of wants to live through us and is always drawing us back into fellowship with him. When this truth "clicks" and the lightbulb goes on in our souls, we can experience Christ's presence in a whole new way as we:

*Live in astonishment.* "Remember the wonders he has done," says 1 Chronicles 16:12 (NIV). As Earl gazed out across the valleys into the distant mountains of Vietnam, he saw more than the external beauty of his surroundings. The trees and flowers, every facet of creation, had become a personal expression of the love of Earl's Maker and Husband (Isa. 54:5) to the Bride, God's people. God wants us to live in this kind of wonder at the majesty and glory displayed in nature.

Are you astonished at the amazing love of your Bridegroom? Have you ever experienced the "deep calling unto deep" (Ps. 42:7) while looking at an awesome aspect of nature—the Grand Canyon, a high mountain peak, or the skies lit up by a brilliant sunset? Has your heart leapt when you saw a multi-colored field of wildflowers or watched the wild breakers of the ocean splash on granite rocks? The next time you're out in nature, even in your own backyard, ask for new eyes not only to see creation as an expression of God's love but also to know the intimacy with him to which his love beckons us.

*Let the truth change your life.* "'No eye has seen, no ear has heard, no mind has conceived what God has prepared for those who love him'—but God has revealed it to us by his Spirit," says 1 Corinthians 2:9–10 (NIV). We tend to interpret these words to mean that we'll see and possess wonderful things in heaven. Although that is true, eternal life is not just a future hope, it is a present reality. "This is eternal life: that they may know you, the only true God, and Jesus Christ, whom you have sent" (John 17:3 NIV). We abide in Jesus and he abides in us by his Spirit, *now*. And he calls to us and demonstrates his love through his very creation. As we meditate on these truths, the Lord will transform our lives.

TWENTY

# The Power
# *of* His Word

*When Jesus Christ utters a word, He opens his mouth*
*so wide that it embraces all heaven and earth, even*
*though that word be but in a whisper.*

MARTIN LUTHER

M
ary passed the entrances of the market stalls that
clamored for her coins. The smells of the busy
metropolis, Magdala, once tantalized her but now
nauseated her. She pushed harder, hoping to make it home
before . . .

No! She wouldn't dwell on that. If she concentrated on
the tasks of her day, perhaps the enemies of her mind might

give her respite. Yet only yesterday she had found herself in the darkness once again. Mary closed her eyes as she tried to erase the memory of the horrified looks of the innocent bystanders who stared down upon her. She pressed harder toward home.

Home! Mary quickened her pace as the familiar doorway beckoned. She nearly ran through the door into the shadowy sanctuary. Long ago she had ordered the servants to block out unwanted light. She nearly tripped over the young servant girl who stood in the entrance. The girl anxiously looked upon Mary's face and then broke into a smile when she saw her mistress's eyes.

*Sanity,* Mary thought, grimacing. *That's what she hoped to see in my face. Even my own servants don't know whom they will encounter from day to day.* She knew she vacillated between severe lows and highs, experiencing spells of panic or despair, but she had no way to stop the terrible torment afflicting her soul. Mary handed her purchases to the young girl and then slipped into her bedchamber. She lay down and pulled the luxurious bedcovering over her entire body. *Maybe if I sleep, I will be spared.* Tears ran down her cheeks and soaked her pillow. The unwanted voices seeped into her thoughts and she curled into a tight ball, defenseless against the angst that washed over her like crashing waves.

"What is happening to me?" Mary whispered as she spiraled down into blackness and fear. She felt hands clawing at her and shrieked in terror. She tried to push away from something soft and suffocating that strangled her as she writhed. "Help me," she screamed silently, mouthing the words.

"Mary! Mary! Please, it's me." The tender voice penetrated her dark world as Mary arched one way and then the other, thrashing about and reaching with everything within her to find that safe place she desperately needed. "Mary, you're tangled in your bedcovers. Please stop fighting me. Let me help you," the voice said.

Mary gazed into the face of her longtime friend Lydia, who perched on the edge of the bed and clasped Mary's hands against her cheek. The servant girl stood behind her trembling.

"Come out of bed," Lydia said. "Your headdress is a mess, and you've scratched yourself. Girl, please help me," she ordered the servant. They each took one arm to help Mary out of bed and seat her in a chair. The servant removed Mary's headdress, picked up a brush, and began to run it through Mary's long, disheveled hair. Deeply saddened by the sight of the glazed-over eyes and sunken cheeks of her once-attractive friend, Lydia poured water on a clean cloth and bathed the scratches that ran down Mary's face. "You have hurt yourself again," she said. "Were you having a nightmare?"

"You know it was not a nightmare," Mary said. She wrenched away the cloth and threw it to the floor. Cupping her face in her hands and hiding her face in shame, she groaned, "I don't know what to do. I can't go on living like this."

"She hasn't eaten in days," the servant girl said. Her voice quaked with fear. "I bring food to her and she leaves it by the side of the bed uneaten. We don't know what to do. That's why I called for you."

Mary looked up in surprise at the young girl's bravery and saw adoration in her eyes.

"I am glad you sent for me," Lydia said. "We must get Mary to a physician. She is ill."

Mary pushed her friend away gently. "No, Lydia. It's more than that. Something has possessed my mind. At times I feel as if something—or someone—is tormenting me, trying to destroy me." Mary grabbed at Lydia's sleeve. "I cannot go on like this," she said. "I don't know where to turn."

Lydia sat in silence, staring at her friend. Mary knew that she was shocked at her appearance. She could no longer bear to look upon her own image because the hollow-eyed, stark woman she had become was so different from who she used to be. She saw the helplessness in her friend's eyes.

"May I make a suggestion?" the servant girl asked. "I've heard of a teacher who is also a healer." The young girl smiled and suddenly looked beautiful. "He has healed many," she continued. "His teachings are profound and his miracles even greater. He has stirred up the religious men in the community who do not know what to do with him or the crowds who follow him as he teaches. He ministers to both the rich and the poor. He heals the sick and the lame." She paused. "I've heard that he is in Capernaum, only three miles from here. We could be there within the hour if we left right now."

Lydia scoffed. "A religious teacher? My friend needs a doctor, not some traveling holy man. Please. I appreciate what you have done for Mary, but you are overstepping your bounds."

The servant girl whispered, "Just the other day Jesus healed a woman who suffered like my mistress does. Her name is Joanna."

"Joanna the wife of Cuza?" Mary asked. She had heard the rumors. They had said she was mad. Something sparked in Mary's soul. She wrapped her headdress around her face to hide the deep scratches in her flesh. "Let's go now," she said and rushed from the room.

Mary, Lydia, and the servant girl approached Capernaum. As they traveled along the coast of Galilee, Mary stopped everyone she encountered to ask if they knew where to find the teacher. Lydia begged her to turn around and return home but wouldn't leave the side of her friend. Suddenly Mary stopped and shaded her eyes, looking into the distance. A crowd had gathered at the shore. "There!" she said. "I think it is the teacher. I must go to him." She grabbed Lydia's hand and broke into a run.

A man stood on the deck of a small fishing boat. Twelve men stood around him as he taught. "I'm sorry," the man said. "I must go, but I will come back tomorrow." He smiled at the crowd on the shore and they broke into cheers. Not far away stood three Pharisees, their frowns of disapproval lost on the rowdy crowd.

"Wait," Mary cried. She pushed through the crowd, trying to get to the teacher. Lydia grabbed at Mary's robe, but Mary pushed her friend's hand away and rushed forward. "Please wait for me," she said.

Surrounded by his followers, the teacher turned and looked at her. It seemed as if he saw into her soul. Mary staggered as the darkness inside tried to push her to the ground. Panic gripped her heart. She had to leave now. Why had she been so foolish to think that a simple teacher could help her? She turned and stumbled as people parted.

Her servant ran to her side and locked her arm around her waist. "I will help you find your way to the teacher," she said. "Please don't give up." The girl waved her arm in the air. "Jesus, my mistress needs a miracle!" Mary staggered under the weight of the insanity that threatened to envelope her. Then she heard the voice.

The teacher's robe was wet where he had plunged into the shallows of the seashore. "Leave her," he said quietly. "You have no authority."

Mary closed her eyes, sinking into the darkness. "Leave her! Go back to your native hell, you foul spirits from the pit!" the teacher said again as he touched her. Seven times she felt a piercing light as the power of his words rebuked the tormenting demons. Then peace washed over her body and mind like the lapping water that etched the sand below her feet.

Mary opened her eyes and the golden light of the sun revealed the Master smiling at her. "You are healed, my sister," he said. Sanity returned to her and a rosy tint returned to her cheeks as she was made whole.[1] Mary fell to her knees in the sand and wept with joy.

In the weeks after her miraculous encounter with Jesus, Mary sat at his feet in adoration. She discovered that the teacher was the long-awaited Messiah, and she gladly followed him from town to town. She and other women of means, like Joanna and Susanna, shared their money and spent their time ministering to Jesus and his disciples.

But the religious leaders' hostility toward Jesus rose, and they eventually arrested her dear friend. She watched in Pilate's hall as the ruthless Pharisees demanded the blood of the Savior who was so precious to her. She listened, heartsick, as Pilate read the death sentence. She wept bitterly as Jesus was dragged from the hall and spat upon and abused by the crowd.[2]

Then she knelt at a rugged cross. "Jesus," she whispered, too broken to gaze at the Messiah. His blood dripped to the ground. Most of the disciples had abandoned him, fleeing into the night to save themselves, and the Roman soldiers stood nearby, their swords at ready to kill any who attempted to help Jesus. Mary knew that her allegiance to the Master could cost her everything—her reputation, her very life—but she didn't care. She stood right beside his mother, faithful to the end.

In her darkest hour, he had given her life. Therefore in his darkest hour, she would remain at the foot of the cruel cross no matter what the cost.

"I love you, my Lord," she whispered, her heart torn with love for the one who had set her free.

On the third day after Jesus' death, Mary Magdalene was the first to arrive at the tomb in the garden. As the first light of dawn broke through, she cautiously looked inside the cave where the Messiah's body had been laid after she, Joseph, and Nicodemus had prepared it for burial. Two white-robed angels were sitting where Jesus' body had been laid.

"Woman, why do you weep?" the angels asked Mary.

"They took my Master," she replied, trembling, "and I don't know where they put him." Then she turned and saw Jesus standing there, but she didn't recognize him.

Jesus asked her, "Woman, why do you weep? Who are you looking for?"

Thinking he was just the gardener, she said, "Mister, if you took him, tell me where you put him so I can care for him."

"Mary," Jesus said.

The familiar gentle tone of his voice gripped her heart, and she turned to him and said in Hebrew, "Rabboni!" which means "Teacher!"

He said, "Don't cling to me, for I haven't yet ascended to the Father. Go to my brothers and tell them, 'I ascend to my Father and your Father, my God and your God.'"

Mary Magdalene ran from the tomb, telling the news to every disciple she saw. "I have seen the Lord! I have seen the Lord!" she cried, and she shared everything he had said to her.[3]

# Catching a Fresh Vision of Jesus

Many people, like Mary Magdalene, are tormented—and demons or no demons, Jesus can change their lives forever. Mary was completely powerless over the tormenting spirits that afflicted her, and she needed a Savior and Deliverer whose power was greater than the enemy. We can't tell the depressed or desperate person to just "get a grip," "buck up and things will get better," or "improve your attitude and choose happiness" any more than Mary's servant and friend could tell her to snap out of her dark spells of insanity and expect her to do it.

The Bible doesn't tell us whether Mary inherited a genetic tendency toward mental illness, a dramatic event triggered it, or it was caused by a chemical imbalance. According to Dr. Herbert Lockyer, author of *All the Women of the Bible*, who is considered an expert on biblical characters and history, Mary Magdalene was deeply afflicted and suffered from periodic insanity because of demonic bondage.[4] We do know that with a few words from Jesus, Mary was set free forever to love and serve the Messiah. What a wonderful thing that although others saw a deranged woman, Jesus saw in Mary "the ministering angel who would be a blessing to his own heart and others'."[5]

Mary's healing didn't come from self-analysis; it came from an encounter with the living Lord. And he is just as available and powerful to defeat the powers of darkness in our lives today if we simply come to him and submit ourselves to his authority. Mary's life reveals how you and I can enter into a life-changing intimacy with Christ, and in doing so, see and experience fresh glimpses of the love and glory of our Savior.

*When you are troubled, depressed, or oppressed, allow Jesus's words to nourish and heal your soul.* Invite his Spirit to help you in your weakness and show you what to pray for since "the Spirit himself intercedes for you with groans that words cannot express" (Rom. 8:26 NIV). Don't wait until you "feel like it" to get help from others—move toward other believers for worship, fellowship, and help in your time of need. At the same time let me encourage you to remember the value of medical attention and psychological counseling besides spiritual solutions when it is needed. God uses people in different caring professions as well as in the church to bring relief and healing.

*Spend time with Jesus.* "Mary Magdalene had the priceless privilege of being a member of Jesus' traveling team," said Vickey Banks in *Sharing His Secrets.*[6] Mary didn't just have a one-time power encounter with Christ, receive deliverance and healing, and then run into the sunset to pursue her own happiness. She was willing to lose her life for the one who had given her life. She gave Jesus "her time, her money, and her unwavering devotion. And it all happened during their day-to-day travels together."[7]

Likewise, we need to take time to develop a close relationship with Jesus and to really know him, not just know about him. Not out of legalistic duty or obligation, but out of love for Jesus. We need time to learn to hear his voice ourselves, so that it becomes familiar to us, instead of just hearing what other people say about him. Our prayer often consists of making some fervent requests and then running out to take care of our to-do list for the day instead of waiting on God. But, as Vickey Banks says, "It takes time. Intimacy with God happens as the result of daily deciding to walk and talk with Him."[8]

Like Mary, we can make it our purpose to know the Lord intimately by walking and talking with him throughout our busy days. He wants prayer to be not just a pit stop for spiritual refueling in the morning but a continual dialogue that turns the salvation experience into a life-giving relationship with the living Lord. We don't have to be seated in a pew to experience him. He invites us to practice his presence moment by moment on our journey through life, meditating on his words recorded in the Gospels and talking and listening to him as we work, drive, walk, and tuck our kids into bed. In so doing, the power of his word will bless and enrich our lives over and over again.

# TWENTY-ONE

# The Miracle
# *of* His Presence

*God's end is the process—that I see Him walking on*
*the waves, no shore in sight, no success, no goal, just*
*the absolute certainty that it is all right because I see*
*Him walking on the sea. It is the process, not the end,*
*which is glorifying to God.*

OSWALD CHAMBERS

Tonight a big group of Dutch young people is being
put on a train and sent away," Corrie ten Boom heard
someone say in the soup line of Ravensbruck concentration camp.

"Maybe they are going to be sent to a factory, another
concentration camp, or even their deaths," another woman
whispered.

As Corrie prayed for the boys and girls, God showed her what to do. That night she crawled out the window of the washroom and hid in the shadows where she thought the prisoners would pass. All was silent except for the sound of a guard's boot crunching on gravel as he got closer. She heard low moans from the barracks as the searchlight from the tower house swept across the prison grounds. Knowing she would be beaten senseless or killed if she was discovered by the guards, Corrie didn't turn back. She knelt in the dark and asked God to give her a personal word for each and every person being transported.

As they walked by her, Corrie whispered a personal message to each of the 250 young people who passed by her in the dark:

"Jesus is Victor."

"Fear not, only believe."

"Underneath are the everlasting arms."

After the war, one of those young people told Corrie that all but one of the 250 who were transported that night survived and how God had powerfully used Corrie's words to bring them peace not only that night but through the trials, bombing, and dangers they later faced.[1]

This lifestyle of talking and listening to Jesus was a vital part of what prepared Corrie for the suffering she faced in Ravensbruck, called the "Concentration Camp of No Return," when she and her older sister Betsie were imprisoned by the Nazis for hiding and aiding Jews.

In prison prayer was her lifeline, and time after time hearing the voice of her Lord brought hope to Corrie, her sister Betsie, and many other women. One of the first such times came when they first arrived at Ravensbruck. Prisoners were stripped of every possession and made to walk naked into the showers before having prison clothes issued to them. Surrendering her clothes was hard enough, but Corrie knew she couldn't live without her Bible.

Asking the Lord to give her courage, he gave her the idea to wrap her small Bible in her woolen underwear and hide it in a bug-infested corner of the shower room. After showering she stuck the Bible and underwear beneath her prison dress. A few moments later she passed by the inspection station but wasn't stopped. Every single prisoner in front of and behind her was searched, including her sister, but Corrie went by untouched and her Bible went undiscovered by the guards.

Daily the women faced suffering, torment, and cruelty. But that little Bible brought life to hundreds in the barracks as Corrie and Betsie twice daily read God's Word aloud. Corrie was already in her fifties and Betsie was several years older when they entered the concentration camp, and they endured atrocities as did all those at Ravensbruck. They stood outside in the freezing cold without coat or covering for roll call before daybreak every day. They did backbreaking work and had nothing of their own—except the beloved Bible.

Because of rampant fleas, guards wouldn't go in the barracks, so Corrie and Betsie were able to teach others from her secret Bible. As they taught and encouraged the women through Bible studies and church services, many came into a personal relationship with Christ. Even though they lived close to death, the river of life flowed through them.

"They were services like no others . . . in Barracks 28," Corrie wrote in *The Hiding Place.*

A single meeting night might include a recital of the *Magnificat* in Latin by a group of Roman Catholics, a whispered hymn by some Lutherans, and a sotto-voce chant by Eastern Orthodox women. With each moment the crowd around us would swell, packing the nearby platforms, hanging over the edges, until the high structures groaned and swayed.

At last either Betsie or I would open the Bible. Because only the Hollanders could understand the Dutch text we translated aloud in German. And then we would hear the life-giving words passed back along the aisles in French, Polish, Russian, Czech, back into Dutch. They were little previews of heaven, these evenings beneath the light bulb. . . . And I would know again that in darkness God's truth shines most clear.[2]

Over time Betsie grew weaker and became critically ill. One morning she and Corrie walked around the prison grounds at 4:30 A.M. to pray, as they often did before registration. The stench of death stung their nostrils. Darkness and despair hung like a shroud over the camp. Both were weakened by malnutrition and disease, and they were not exempt from discouragement. *How will I go on without my sister and the wisdom she shares with me?* Corrie thought as she wrapped her arms around Betsie. *What about Betsie's dreams of making a house in Holland where people can rebuild their lives after being in concentration camps, her vision of our traveling around the world to tell people what God taught us in prison? Will we ever get out of this horror and back to Holland?*

As they walked in the cold, they felt the presence of Jesus as if he were there and speaking aloud. Betsie would say something, then Corrie would say something, and then the Lord would say something—and both sisters heard what he said. It was an unexplainable but wonderful miracle.[3]

Hearing the Lord speak in this way gave Corrie a whole new vision of Jesus that lifted her gaze above the suffering and horrors of Ravensbruck to the glory of heaven and our eternal hope:

> We saw then that even though everything was terrible, we could rely on the fact that God did not have any problems, only plans. There is never panic in heaven! You can only hold on to that reality through faith because it seemed then, and often seems now, as if the devil is the victor. But God is faithful, and His plans never fail! He knows the future. He knows the way.[4]

Nothing had changed in their circumstances. Everything was still so terrible Corrie thought it couldn't get any worse. They were still "prisoners of people trained in cruelty" and saw no outward sign of hope in that desperate place. Yet they experienced a profound peace as the Lord spoke to them. Singing quiet hymns of praise, they returned to the barracks to strengthen and comfort the women with the comfort they'd received.

Soon Betsie's legs became paralyzed and her body so weak Corrie had to take her to the infirmary. After only two days she died, and her body was dumped together with hundreds of other corpses.

In an amazing turn of events, Corrie was released from Ravensbruck on New Year's Day of 1945, only a few days after Betsie's death. She found out later that God had used an error in the prison paperwork to free her, and at the end of the very week she was released, an order was given to kill all women her age and older.[5]

Corrie was weak, dirty, and hungry, yet on the train back to Holland after her release, she vowed to God that "she would take the message of His love wherever He wanted her to go."[6] She was elderly and her health was broken by the ravages of the concentration camp, but her spirit was strong, and she gave herself anew to Jesus to go wherever he directed and to do whatever he desired.

For more than thirty years after World War II, Corrie was a "Tramp for the Lord" in more than sixty countries and on every continent. She listened for God's marching orders, and then whether it was Africa, South America, or Japan, she went and spoke to people in churches, in prisons, in hospitals, and on college campuses. She believed with all her heart the words of Jeremiah 33:3, which she called "God's Private Telephone Number," in which God says, "Call to Me and I will answer you, and I will tell you great and mighty things, which you do not know" (NASB). God spoke. Corrie listened. As a result, millions heard the message of God's love and forgiveness through meetings, a major movie about her life, her books, and broadcasts on television and radio.

## Catching a Fresh Vision of Jesus

Seeing Jesus is vital for the Christian, Corrie ten Boom believed, because "we are not ready for the battle until we have seen the Lord, for Jesus is the answer to all problems."[7] She had looked in the face of death in a Nazi concentration camp. She had seen the enemy up close. "I saw myself and I saw the devil," she said, "and the devil was much stronger than I. But I saw Jesus too, and Jesus was much stronger than the evil one. Because I was on Jesus' side, I was more than a conqueror! We must never forget that Jesus is always conqueror, and that we just need to be in the right relationship with Him; then His victorious life flows through us and touches others. We can never expect too much of the Lord. Hallelujah, what a Savior!"[8]

What situation makes it difficult for you to be an over-comer? Are you in right relationship with Jesus so his victorious life can flow through you and touch others? If not, you can ask him to forgive your sins and to live in your heart. He has such a great love that we can all come to him and gain a fresh vision of Jesus through his presence in our lives.

Corrie ten Boom's story also encourages us to:

*Gain God's perspective.* More than anything else, Corrie reminds us how vital it is to see things from God's perspective. If we look from underneath our problems and tragedies, we will sink in despair. But if we look to the Lord and gain his perspective, it will make all the difference.[9] Corrie didn't say that glibly, for she *had* been through difficulties greater than any of us can imagine. Yet none of her trials touched the clear vision Corrie had of God's complete faithfulness, of his mercy, and especially of God as her hiding place in the best and worst of times. How do we maintain this kind of focus when everything seems out of control?

We focus on God by hiding the words of Scripture in our hearts as Corrie did. We can cling to words such as 2 Corinthians 4:17–18, which says, "For our present troubles are quite small and won't last very long. Yet they produce for us an immeasurably great glory that will last forever! So we don't look at the troubles we can see right now; rather, we look forward to what we have not yet seen. For the troubles we see will soon be over, but the joys to come will last forever."

*Ask the Lord for a word from the Bible both for yourself and to encourage other people.* Jesus said his sheep would hear his voice (John 10:27), and that is true whether his sheep is a Dutch woman in a concentration camp or you or me. What a wonderful invitation we have in verses like Jeremiah 33:3 that assure us when we call, God will answer! The Lord of the heavens and the earth wants to speak to us and direct our lives. And as you seek him he *will* give you a word of encouragement for your friend, your child, or somebody you meet on the street.

How do we hear his voice in the noisy environment of earth? F. B. Meyer suggested, "Be still each day for a short time, sitting before God in meditation, and ask the Holy Spirit to reveal to you the truth of Christ's indwelling. Ask God to be pleased to make known to you what is the riches of the glory of this mystery (Col. 1:27)."[10] If we carve out a little time for stillness as a part of our lifestyle, then when a situation arises in which we really need to hear from God, we'll be tuned in to him.

God is on the edge of his throne eagerly waiting to reveal himself to you. All of heaven is waiting expectantly for you to ask for a fresh vision of Jesus that will change your life. As we've seen demonstrated through the true stories in this book, it's not enough for us to just know about Jesus or fill our minds with knowledge about the wonders he used to do in Bible days or what he did for us long ago. What we need is to enter into a life-transforming relationship with Jesus by experiencing him, having living interaction with him, and seeing him in our everyday lives. The results are more than worth it. As Oswald Chambers said, "When once you have seen Jesus, you can never be the same."[11]

We have only scratched the suface of the nature, character, and beauty of Christ. As long as we're on this earth, we see through a glass darkly (1 Cor. 13:12 KJV), but one day we will see him face-to-face! My hope is that a longing has grown in you, as it has in me, to more clearly see Jesus, our Redeemer, Savior, Life-giving Lord, and then live "in all the fresh remembrance of the whole"[12] of Christ's love and character.

Some of the people you've read about here were burdened and heartbroken, but one look at Jesus brought new life. Others walked in darkness, but just a few words from the Lord ushered them into his marvelous light. Still others began a deeper spiritual walk, were empowered for ministry, or began living a victorious life from gaining a vision of God. Newness of faith, newness of understanding, newness of life—how we need all three!

If we ask for a fresh vision each day, the Lord will reveal himself in the ordinary things of life—through his Word, people we meet who point us to him, his whispers, creation, a supernatural dream, the most humble acts of service, mountaintop experiences, and the deepest of valleys and trials. In fact, it's often in our most extreme need and the muck and mire of life that God is seen the best. In the darkest places his light shines the brightest. And he is no respecter of persons—what he did for all the people in this book and countless believers throughout history, he'll do for you.

God's Word tells us that he always rewards those who look for him. "You will seek me and find me when you seek me with all your heart. I will be found of you" (Jer. 29:13–14 NIV).

Would you pray with me?

Today, Lord, I want to see you. I want to know you more! Open the eyes of my heart. Open my spiritual ears so I can hear your voice. As I walk with you through my daily life, let me see your hand at work and experience the fulfillment of your promise in John 10:10: "life in all its fullness"! Amen.

# Notes

## Chapter 1: Seeing Jesus

1. Quoted in *One Holy Passion,* ed. and comp. Judith Couchman (Colorado Springs: WaterBrook Press, 1998), 75–76.

2. Oswald Chambers, *My Utmost for His Highest* (Westwood, NJ: Dodd, Mead, & Company, Inc., 1935), 100.

## Chapter 2: The Living Word

1. Edith Schaeffer, "God's Definition of Faith," in Couchman, *One Holy Passion,*154.

2. Josh McDowell, *Beyond Belief to Conviction* (Wheaton: Tyndale House, 2002), 209, 224.

3. Madame Guyon, "Excerpts from Experiencing the Depths of Jesus Christ," in Richard J. Foster and James Bryan Smith, *Devotional Classics* (San Francisco: HarperSanFrancisco, 1993), 321–23.

## Chapter 3: The Psalms Prescription

1. Chambers, *My Utmost for His Highest.*

## Chapter 4: Words That Changed a Life

1. The dialogue has been quoted or adapted from John 4, *The Message*.

2. Herbert Lockyer, *All The Women of the Bible* (Grand Rapids: Zondervan, 1968), 239.

3. Chambers, *My Utmost for His Highest*, 244.

## Chapter 5: A Vision That Endures

1. Letter of Hannah Whitall Smith to Priscilla Mounsey, January 1, 1882, quoted in Marie Henry, *Hannah Whitall Smith* (Minneapolis: Bethany, 1984), 104.

2. Hannah Whitall Smith, *The Unselfishness of God* (Princeton, NJ: Littlebrook Publishing, Inc., 1987), 21.

3. Ibid., 23.

4. Ibid., 131.

5. Hannah Whitall Smith, quoted in Henry, *Hannah Whitall Smith*, 30.

6. Smith, *The Unselfishness of God*, 11.

7. Ibid., 141.

8. Ibid., 151.

9. Ibid., 152.

10. Ibid., 151.

11. Ibid., 153.

12. Henry, *Hannah Whitall Smith*, 34.

13. Smith, *The Unselfishness of God*, 137.

14. Ibid., 163, 170.

15. Hannah Whitall Smith, *God Is Enough* (New York: Ballantine/Epiphany Books, 1992), 26.

16. Henry, *Hannah Whitall Smith*, 43.

17. Ibid., 46.

18. Smith, *The Unselfishness of God*, 164–65.

19. Hannah Whitall Smith, *The Christian's Secret of a Happy Life* (Westwood, NJ: Fleming H. Revell Co., 1952), 246.

20. Ibid., 239.

21. Ibid., 243.

22. Smith, *Unselfishness of God,* 165.

23. Smith, *God Is Enough,* 274.

24. Ibid., 247.

## Chapter 7: The Face of Jesus

1. Mother Teresa, *Total Surrender* (Ann Arbor, MI: Servant Publications, 1985), 118.

2. Mother Teresa, *Works of Love, Works of Peace* (San Francisco: Ignatius Press, 1996), 35.

3. Mother Teresa, *In My Own Words* (Liguori, MO: Liguori Publications, 1989), 52.

4. J. B. Phillips, 120.

## Chapter 8: An Expectant Heart

1. Lockyer, *All the Women of the Bible,* 30.

2. Ibid., 30.

3. Ibid., 31.

4. Ibid., 30.

5. Ibid., 31.

## Chapter 9: Jehovah Is Still God

1. Mark Robson, director, Alan Burgess and Isabel Lennart, scriptwriters, *The Inn of the Sixth Happiness,* 20th Century Fox, 1958.

2. Catherine Swift, *Gladys Aylward* (Minneapolis: Bethany, 1984, 1989), 17–39.

3. Alan Burgess, *The Small Woman* (New York: Dutton, 1957), 47, 95–107.

4. Ibid., 122.

5. Ibid., 225.

6. Bill Hybels, *The God You're Looking For* (Nashville: Thomas Nelson, 1997), 85.

## Chapter 10: Climbing into God's Lap

1. Anne Graham Lotz, "My Heart's Cry," *Fresh Outlook*, November/December 2003, 46.

2. J. B. Phillips, *Your God Is Too Small* (New York: Macmillan, 1961), 33.

3. Jack Frost, "Come Home to the Father," *Charisma*, October 2002, 99–101.

4. Cindy Crosby, "America's Pastor," *Christianity Today*, March 2004, 61.

5. I wish to express my appreciation for the works of Paula and John Sandford and their audiotape "How We See God," which brought more insight to this subject.

## Chapter 11: The Lord Who Sees Me

1. If you would like to hear more of Terri Geary's inspirational testimony, you may contact her at terriorrgeary@juno.com.

2. Charles Spurgeon, "God's Omniscience," *Classic Sermons on the Attributes of God,* comp. Warren W. Wiersbe (Grand Rapids: Kregel, 1989), 127–28.

3. Ibid., 118.

## Chapter 12: I've Just Seen Jesus!

1. The dialogue has been quoted or adapted from John 11:1–44, *The Message.*

2. Thomas Kelly, "Excerpts from *A Testament of Devotion*," in Richard J. Foster and James Bryan Smith, *Devotional Classics* (San Francisco: HarperSanFrancisco, 1993), 208.

3. Corrie ten Boom, *Reflections of His Glory* (Grand Rapids: Zondervan, 1999), 21, 23.

4. Lockyer, *All the Women of the Bible*, 90–91.

## Chapter 13: The Joy of Obedience

1. Hannah Hurnard, *The Hearing Heart* (Wheaton: Tyndale, 1978), 21, 14.

2. Ibid., 24.

3. Ibid., 30.

4. Ibid., 26.

5. Ibid., 26–27.

6. Ibid., 29.

7. A. W. Tozer, *The Pursuit of God* (Camp Hill, PA: Christian Publications, 1982), 58–59.

8. Hurnard, *The Hearing Heart*, 111–39.

## Chapter 14: The Great Physician

1. Richard Foster, *Prayer: Finding the Heart's True Home* (San Francisco: Harper Collins, 1992), 203.

## Chapter 15: A Light in the Darkness

1. Chambers, *My Utmost for His Highest*, 100.

2. Lee Strobel, *The Case for Faith: Student Edition* (Grand Rapids: Zondervan, 2002), 59.

## Chapter 16: The Road to Emmaus

1. The dialogue has been quoted or adapted from Luke 24, *The Message*.

2. Phillips Brooks, quoted in Edythe Draper, *Draper's Book of Quotations for the Christian World* (Wheaton: Tyndale, 1992), 347, entry 6381.

## Chapter 17: The Trysting Place

1. Charlie Riggs, *Practicing His Presence* (Asheville, NC: Billy Graham Evangelistic Association, 1995), 5–6.
2. Jim Craddock, *Update*. Oklahoma City: Scope Ministries, August 2003, 1.

## Chapter 19: Can You Hear My Voice?

1. George MacDonald, quoted in Draper, *Draper's Book of Quotations,* 109.

## Chapter 20: The Power of His Word

1. Lockyer, *All the Women of the Bible,* 101.
2. Ibid., 101–02.
3. The dialogue has been quoted or adapted from John 20, *The Message.*
4. Lockyer, *All the Women of the Bible,* 100–101.
5. Ibid., 100.
6. Vickey Banks, *Sharing His Secrets: Intimate Insights from the Women Who Knew Jesus* (Portland, OR: Multnomah Publishers, 2001), 182–83.
7. Ibid., 183.
8. Ibid.

## Chapter 21: The Miracle of His Presence

1. Carole C. Carlson, *Corrie ten Boom: Her Life, Her Faith* (Grand Rapids: Revell, 1983), 116–21.

2. Corrie ten Boom, *The Hiding Place* (New York: Bantam Books, 1971), 201.

3. Corrie ten Boom, *Reflections of His Glory* (Grand Rapids: Zondervan, 1999), 92.

4. Ibid., 92.

5. Ibid., 11.

6. Carlson, *Corrie ten Boom*, 121.

7. Ten Boom, *Reflections of His Glory*, 92.

8. Ibid., 100–101.

9. Ibid., 91–92.

10. F. B. Meyer, *The Secret of Guidance* (Chicago: Moody, 1997), 43.

11. Chambers, *My Utmost for His Highest*, 100.

12. Wiersbe, *Classic Sermons*, 86.

**Cheri Fuller** is an international speaker and award-winning author of over thirty books including *Fearless: Building a Faith That Overcomes Your Fear,* the best-selling *When Mothers Pray,* and *The One Year Book of Praying through the Bible.* Fuller is a prolific author who has written hundreds of articles for *Focus on the Family, Moody, Family Circle, Guideposts, Pray!* Magazine, and many others. She has been a frequent guest on national radio and TV programs including *Focus on the Family, At Home—Live!, Moody Midday Connection,* and many others.

Cheri's ministry, Families Pray USA, inspires and equips women, children, teens, and churches to impact their world through prayer. She is a contributing writer for *Today's Christian Woman,* and her website, www.CheriFuller.com, features her column "Mothering by Heart," resources on prayer and inspiration. She and her husband live in Oklahoma.

To schedule Cheri for speaking engagements or conferences, contact Speak Up Speaker Services at (810) 982-0898 or speakupinc@aol.com